DAVID~
Good luck in
the ad wars!

Best,

The Little Blue
Book of Advertising

PORTFOLIO

The Little Blue Book of Advertising

FIFTY-TWO

SMALL

IDEAS

THAT CAN

MAKE A

BIG

DIFFERENCE

STEVE LANCE AND JEFF WOLL

PORTFOLIO

PORTFOLIO

Published by the Penguin Group

Penguin Group (USA) Inc., 375 Hudson Street, New York, New York 10014, U.S.A.
Penguin Group (Canada), 90 Eglinton Avenue East, Suite 700, Toronto,
Ontario, Canada M4P 2Y3 (a division of Pearson Penguin Canada Inc.)
Penguin Books Ltd, 80 Strand, London WC2R 0RL, England
Penguin Ireland, 25 St. Stephen's Green,
Dublin 2, Ireland (a division of Penguin Books Ltd)
Penguin Books Australia Ltd, 250 Camberwell Road, Camberwell, Victoria 3124,
Australia (a division of Pearson Australia Group Pty Ltd)
Penguin Books India Pvt Ltd, 11 Community Centre,
Panchsheel Park, New Delhi – 110 017, India
Penguin Group (NZ), Cnr Airborne and Rosedale Roads, Albany, Auckland 1310,
New Zealand (a division of Pearson New Zealand Ltd)
Penguin Books (South Africa) (Pty) Ltd, 24 Sturdee Avenue, Rosebank,
Johannesburg 2196, South Africa

Penguin Books Ltd, Registered Offices:
80 Strand, London WC2R 0RL, England

First published in 2006 by Portfolio,
a member of Penguin Group (USA) Inc.

1   3   5   7   9   10   8   6   4   2

Page 270 constitutes an extension of this copyright page.

Publisher's Note
This publication is designed to provide accurate and authoritative information in
regard to the subject matter covered. It is sold with the understanding that the
publisher is not engaged in rendering legal, accounting or other professional services. If you require legal advice or other expert assistance, you should seek the
services of a competent professional.

ISBN 1-59184-124-0

Printed in the United States of America
Set in Minion • Designed by Elke Sigal

To Ellen, Ben, and Becky
who supported and shared my many adventures
—Jeff

To Max and Dan, who keep me young in spite of myself
—Steve

Contents

Section Six:
TV Commercials

Section Seven:
Print Advertising

Section Eight:
The Internet

Section Nine:
Radio, Outdoor, and Direct Response

Section Ten:
On the Set

Section Eleven:
Bonus

Introduction

HOW COME ALL THE GREAT ADVERTISING YOU LIKE ISN'T yours?

Why do your smart, insightful promotion and marketing ideas somehow turn into mush by the time they're executed? If they're executed at all. And isn't "executed" an interesting turn of phrase? How appropriate.

If you're a marketer, how come your agency isn't giving you the kind of work you saw in their pitch to you?

If you're a creative director, how come you seem to have the title—but not the job?

If you're a copywriter, art director, or designer (no matter the medium you work in), how come your best work isn't shown to the client—and is rarely approved?

The reason your advertising isn't working is that your processes for creating and producing great advertising aren't working. To quote William Shakespeare (and if you're going to write a book, who better to quote?), "The fault, dear Brutus, is not in our stars, But in ourselves . . ."

In the 1990s, the world economy (and particularly the U.S. economy) experienced the greatest economic expansion in recorded history. New millionaires were being created almost as fast as new jobs were. New companies were launching—and spending tens of millions of dollars to promote themselves. One of our clients observed, "Everyone looks like a strong swimmer when the tide's coming in." And in the 1990s, everyone looked like a strong swimmer.

But along came the dot-com bust—and with it, a lot of excuses why your advertising and marketing wasn't as effective as you wanted it to be.

"The Internet is revolutionizing advertising!"

"Network TV is doomed!"

"Magazines are dying!"

"Free radio is dead!"

"Madison Avenue is a dinosaur!"

Oh, please. Why not just yell "the sky is falling, the sky is falling" and be done with it?

We've seen recessions.

We've seen the previous death of TV and the rise of cable.

We've seen new audiences and new media come and go.

And through it all, we continue to see good advertising out there that works.

Why? Because there are still people out there who know what to do to make it work.

Once it's in your blood you never get rid of it. The profession of advertising becomes a core component of your psyche, generating tremendous emotional involvement. It becomes intrinsic to your being and means you'll never cease to analyze and critique (and praise) the advertising you see and hear; never stop thinking about new media; never stop trying to determine how to create advertising that increases brand awareness and consumer interest and recall.

We've been doing it separately and together for nearly thirty years. And when we first teamed up, we started asking ourselves whether we could articulate the processes that went into making a great ad.

Steve Lance has spent nearly thirty years in advertising and marketing at advertising agencies and television networks, including Creative Director of NBC; Associate Creative Director of Backer & Spielvogel; and Creative Director of the entertainment division of Della Femina, Travisano & Partners. He's been a Member of the Board of Directors of The Copy Club of New York; a guest lecturer on promotion and advertising at universities, clients and advertising clubs across America; and author of *The 49th Annual of Advertising, Editorial & Television Art and Design* and ghostwriter of the bestseller *It's Your Money—The E*TRADE Guide To Online Investing*. He works with Jeff at Unconventional Wisdom—a creative resource group based on the Internet at www. uwisdom.com.

Jeff Woll was an integral part of the growth and success of Ogilvy & Mather. After years in New York he helped open their Chicago office where he managed over $100 million in billing; he then moved north as Managing Director and COO of their Montreal office. Within eighteen months he rebuilt the creative department, winning multiple creative awards including three gold medals in Quebec's Agency of the Year Awards. He became Managing Director, CEO of Ogilvy & Mather Partners in New York and then head of Corporate Development of O&M, working with the Chairman and Vice Chairman of North America on long-range strategic planning, new technologies, and acquisitions. Jeff eventually led a spin-off from O&M and formed Red Shark Technology, a multimedia computer company that was funded and then acquired by IBM. Jeff is now president of Unconventional Wisdom and active in helping start-up companies.

We went into business together almost fifteen years ago with our art director partner, Norm Siegel. We were introduced by a previous Ogilvy partner of Jeff's, Tina Georgeou, who knew of our common love for great and unexpected creative work and our common search for principles of advertising that would ensure that our clients could count on an efficient and effective iterative process rather than ad hoc guesswork.

Our first corporate workshop was called On-A.I.R. Wisdom™. "A.I.R." was an acronym for the three things any good commercial or promo should do. Get the audience's ATTENTION. Hold their INTEREST. Make them RECALL the message. Simple, no? But it took us almost six months to outline eight steps that could keep a client's promos focused.

"Thank you!"

"Bravo!"

"Would you present this to senior management?"

"Do you have more seminars you can share with us?"

Those were the audience responses to our first seminar—and the usual response we get at the dozens we've developed and presented since. It feels good. Big ego win. You get to show up, stand in front of a room for ninety minutes or two days, be an expert, watch the lights go on in people's eyes—and not have to stay around to clean up the mess.

Yes, a mess. Because we've rarely seen management following through to help their teams and their companies. And we're not talking about the CEO of the corporation. We're talking about department managers and group heads who don't know what it really takes to install and manage a process that can create an environment where great work will be produced.

Somewhere between the nineties' hype, the Internet bubble, and the large layoffs of senior and middle marketing and advertising management, the information presented in this book—much of it timeless—got lost. Poof. Disappeared. So we finally decided to provide the help we've heard actual screams for and write the book our seminar audiences have long requested. Real, usable help. So up-and-coming advertising professionals can do their jobs well today and brilliantly tomorrow. Advice that can let you truly manage your job and your people . . . not just, well, manage to get by.

It's vital, everyday information that you need each and every day on the job. It's information, for the most part, that we were taught day in and day out on our jobs, no matter the company or the industry. But we find that today's marketing and advertising executives just don't have those learning opportunities. Few have been trained well by their supervisors, fewer in formal company classes. And, what's not been taught has not been learned.

We've organized the information for everyday use. For quick reads to specific problems. And we almost guarantee that it will make a big difference in how you approach your day-to-day work, how you do that work, and the results you deliver.

All of you know some of this. Some of you know all of this. All of us forget some of this most of the time. It's mostly a helluva lot of common sense. But as Steve's seventh-grade math teacher used to tell him, "Common sense isn't so common."

POINTS OF VIEW

This book and our business relationships are guided by three key points of view. Think of them as a framework in which all the tips can fit. Adopt them and you and your team will produce better advertising.

1. Marketers and Creatives Don't Speak the Same Language

2. Think Inside the Box

3. You Can't Manage What You Don't Measure

"Let me see the first one again."

POINTS OF VIEW

1

MARKETERS AND CREATIVES DON'T SPEAK THE SAME LANGUAGE

THIS IS AN AGE-OLD PHENOMENON, BUT WE DON'T find many who face up to the fact. As Jerry Della Femina observed in his classic book *From Those Wonderful Folks Who Gave You Pearl Harbor,* it used to be (in those long forgotten dark ages of the 1950s and '60s) that if you had a college degree and looked trustworthy, they made you an account executive. If you had a pencil behind your ear, they made you a copywriter.

Then somewhere in the 1970s, they created a job called "marketer." When Bill Bernbach announced to his agency they were hiring a marketer, one of his creative directors, Norman Tanen, wanted to know if this was a person who was going to do the shopping at lunch hour for the creative people.

At the same time, colleges started awarding degrees for training in the jobs of copywriter, art director, and marketing executive. Suddenly, you needed an MBA to get into a marketing training program—and a BFA to become an art director. Different schools, different training, different language, different jargon.

The differences probably started even earlier. Steve has a theory that you can tell whether a person is a marketer or a creative by asking where they sat in their high school classroom. The front row folks? Agency presidents and brand managers. The ones over by the window staring at the scenery? Directors and art directors. The ones near the door? Copywriters.

Even Jeff admits to a more recent cultural bias. He believes marketers were the cheerleaders or sports team players. The creatives? The ones dressed in black who were shopping for another earring in the mall.

Creatives spent hours experimenting with visuals and games on the computer. Marketers spent time Instant-Messaging friends.

Get the picture? From the start, your worlds were different. There's a huge communications gap between marketers and creatives.

But now you're building a brand as part of a team. Your futures are joined. What are the odds that your brains will work in synch? What are the odds you'll get it all right, right away?

In 1992, John Gray wrote *Men Are from Mars, Women Are from Venus,* an insightful book pointing out the differing thought processes between men and women. In advertising and marketing, these differences seem to be transsexual: "Mars" thinking seems to be marketing-related (MBA). "Venus" thinking seems to be creative-related. Understanding that difference and how to manage it is the heart of this book and will get you great work almost every time. (More on that in later chapters.)

Marketing is linear, literal, and logical. Creative is nonlinear, emotional, and illogical. You need *both* in order to create great advertising. The problems arise when neither the creative team nor the marketing people understand that they're speaking different languages.

Understanding the language gap came out of a meeting Steve had with the creative director of one of our clients and the president of a cable network. The president kept saying she wanted the logo bigger. The creative director kept trying to explain to the president why that wouldn't work. As they got increasingly frustrated with each other, Steve suddenly realized the two people were talking completely different languages: the president was talking "marketing," the creative director was talking "design." From a design point of view, it was clear that making the logo bigger would change the visual center of the ad. But the president had no design training and could never see the point.

Advertising is mainly only words and pictures but you've got to make an extraordinary effort to guide, prod, push, pull your point of view—and then listen, try to understand, and possibly accept the other side's point of view.

Will it work all the time? No. There are creative folk that Jeff could never work well with. There are marketers that Steve loathed and refused to work with. (No names here, but it sometimes was a virtual war with office politics that were downright vicious. Sometimes even involving the client—a worst-case scenario.) But when the whole team clicks the result is usually terrific advertising.

And that's fun. And rewarding. And the whole damned point of the business, isn't it?

"I'll start thinking outside the box when the box is empty."

POINTS OF VIEW

2

THINK INSIDE THE BOX

OVER THE YEARS, WE'VE READ LITERALLY HUN-
dreds of books that, in one form or another, talk
about "the new marketing" and "thinking outside
the box." One-to-one marketing. Tipping points.
Viral marketing. Upping the organization. Shifting corporate culture. Japan, Inc. China, Inc.
There's a vast and growing industry of "paradigm
shift" marketing books devoted to one simple
truth: you're not getting the results you want
from your marketing and advertising. And each
of those paradigm shift books claims to have the
one truth that will revolutionize your business,
create breakthrough marketing and advertising,
and deliver the results you want.

Here's our take on all that:

First, there's no such thing as "new marketing." There may be new ways to reach your target
audience; there may be new media alternatives
and new ways to cut through the clutter; but all

consumers of every age are still motivated by the same things that motivated consumers since the first caveman coveted his neighbor's cudgel: needs, status, a belief that the product will improve the perceived quality of their lives, or just an unexplained "I gotta have that" impulsive action.

Second, thinking outside the box is a pointless exercise. If you're Albert Einstein, go ahead and think outside the box. For us mere mortals, doing something brilliant even within the boxes we know is a rare event. (Steve, by the way, claims to be related to Albert Einstein on his father's side, so we allow him to think outside the box on rare occasions.)

Why would you want to think outside the box anyway? Over the centuries, a lot of smart people have filled a lot of boxes with a lot of good stuff. The problem isn't with what's in the boxes, the problem is that today, few people actually take the time to step back, catch their breath, and ask four key questions:

"What are we doing?"

"How are we doing it?"

"Why are we doing it?"

"How do we know if it's working?"

Ever since marketing and advertising were

defined as the components of selling, some very smart people have spent a lot of time and money asking—and honestly answering—those four simple questions. And over the years, the answers to those questions were passed along from mentor to disciple in simple, easy-to-understand maxims.

Today everyone's groping around for processes and answers. They're turning to new gurus and the latest paradigm shift marketing book in hopes they'll find quick, easy answers.

This isn't one of those books.

Rather, it's the compilation of years of know-how that form a foundation on which you can build a lasting brand, an advertising campaign that works (regardless of your audience), and promotions that produce effective results.

These principles worked for advertisers and marketers one hundred years ago, fifty years ago, ten years ago, and last week. They'll work for you next week, too. No matter how much the world keeps changing.

3

YOU CAN'T MANAGE WHAT YOU DON'T MEASURE

ZEN KOANS ARE THOSE PARADOXES THAT ZEN masters give their disciples to help them move to the Zen state of "no mind." The most well-known one is "You know the sound of two hands clapping. What is the sound of one hand clapping?" Here's the most important koan of this book:

How can you manage what you don't measure?

Is your advertising effective? How do you know? Is your communication cutting-edge? How can you tell? Is your marketing on target? Who says? It doesn't matter what parameters you use, but you've got to agree on a baseline and goal for measurement and comparison. One more time:

You can't manage what you don't measure.

How you measure it is totally up to you. If you're an advertising agency, you might want to measure how many awards your creative people win. Fine. Nothing wrong with that. Awards and trophies look good on the mantelpiece and make the recipients feel acknowledged. Some agencies measure how much billing they've gained in the past year. Others (wisely) prefer to measure clients' spending growth.

As a client, you can do all that and far more. Burke scores. Recall testing. Nielsen measurement. Sales. There are literally hundreds of indices you can use to start to get a baseline on your advertising and then measure against progress as you go along.

Pick one, two, or as many as are realistic or the number you can afford to act on. Then start the measurement process. And don't change parameters in the middle of your measurement schedule. If you're measuring dollar sales one month, don't switch to unit sales the next. Pick the measurement you feel is most realistic and most evergreen and stick with it as long as you can.

Whatever metric you use, give yourself at least a year to track the results. Seasonality will always be a factor in sales. While CFOs, CEOs, and Wall

Street analysts will be pushing you for constantly improving results, taking the long view will give you a more realistic view of the market—and the effect your advertising is having on it.

Besides giving yourself a tool (weapon) you can use with senior management (or you agency), it gives everyone who works for you an objective basis on which they can measure their own growth and success.

If awards are your standards, your agency and in-house people can know on an annual basis if they're doing "better" or "worse" than the year before. If they're not doing as well, you'll know what you have to focus on: "Why didn't we win as many awards?" Suddenly, you have a concrete question that can produce meaningful change. ("Blue was out and blue is our corporate color" might not be the answer you're looking for.)

If recall scores are your standard of measurement, then you can know overnight if your advertising is working. (Why do they call it "recall" scores? Many people think it's because the score is a measurement of how well people remember your message. Jaded creative people say it's because if the number isn't high enough, they're going to recall the work.) And you can start creating ads specifically to generate recall. Mnemonics. Opening hooks. Special effects. Sound effects. You can use every trick in your arsenal to consciously build a commercial people will remember. Of course, that might not sell any product, but at least they'll remember your commercial.

Again, our point here isn't to favor one type of measurement over another. Everyone in your organizational chart—both above and below you—should agree on what the measurement will be and then work together to develop a methodology that will help you improve your score and progress.

Pick your standards. Pick your measurements. Set your standards as high as you dare—then live up to them. If you live up to your standards, it will change not just your advertising, but your life.

KNOW YOUR CUSTOMER, KNOW YOUR BRAND

*"What will it take to put one of you two into a
brand-new Eterna-5000 today?"*

aking care of your brand (building it, managing it, protecting it, and yes, if necessary, reviving it) is the single most important job you've got. Whether you're the president of the company, the EVP of marketing, or the newest employee in the advertising agency's design department.

Your brand will last longer than any of your jobs. It's even likely to last longer than your company. So taking care of your brand is also a smart career move—if you take care of the brand, it'll take care of you. No one ever made the cover of Forbes magazine by getting a raise. But the covers and pages of the business press are filled with people who championed a great brand.

What's the easiest way to take care of your brand? Take care of your customer. Know who she is. What he wants. How she uses—and thinks about—your product, service, brand. It's that simple. And that hard.

1

Know Who
Your Customers Are

DAH. DAH. DAH.

If you're over forty, that line might mean nothing to you. But if you're under forty, you might know it as an insipid little background jingle that helped turn around the Volkswagen brand.

Insipid? Yes. Right on target for their audience? Absolutely. And they did it because they knew who their customer was.

Somewhere between the sixties and the nineties, the generation that wanted to overthrow the establishment *became* the establishment. It's always cool to be a little un-hip. To not go along with the crowd. That was always Volkswagen's appeal. But when the Baby Boomers grew up, the symbol of their hipness in the sixties became the vehicle their kids weren't interested in in the nineties. Until their ad agency got back in touch with the voice of their audience—and created a campaign that spoke in the laid-back, slacker voice that had become cool to GenX.

Knowing your audience is the single most important tip in this book. But it generates yawns. Everyone knows they're supposed to know their audience. Yet it's the single biggest omission we find in advertising campaigns we're asked to critique. How many times do you find yourself asking, "Who the hell are they talking to?"

The start to all great advertising is knowing the customer. It's the basis for all successful selling and the most fundamental step for all aspects of marketing and advertising. Before you can launch a brand or extend its scope, write an ad, shoot a commercial, build a Web site, open a new location, or make any key marketing or advertising decision, you've got to have a clear idea who's really buying what you're selling.

You're thinking, "Know who my customers are? I just paid twenty bucks for this drivel?"

Yes. Because once you know your customer you can find out what they're doing, how they're communicating, how they're relating, and what their interests are. If you know all that, you'll know where to find them. Period. And then you'll know what to say to them once you do.

We've heard from some of you that it's "becoming too hard and expensive to truly find my customer." Media fragmentation, smaller research budgets, and the speed of today's business pace have all made it impractical to spend too much time on this. That's outrageous thinking.

Even if you believe, as some smart marketing guys have long thought, that the customer finds the brand and not vice versa—you just gotta know who's buying your brand.

———

Your marketing plan says your audience is "Single, urban women 18–34," but do you and your team truly know them well enough to win and keep their attention, persuade them, get them to talk about you, close a sale, and then get them to buy again?

To get to know your target market and get into their mindset, ask your team if they can answer these questions definitively.

- Who does our brand appeal to?
- Who make up the majority of our customers? Why?
- What do they know, like, love, or dislike about our product?
- What do they know, like, love, or dislike about our brand?
- Is there a difference? How do we know that?

Because there's no longer a "one-size-fits-all" marketing solution, asking these questions is becoming ever more important. Do your homework and you're on the way to getting control of your brand.

There are two ways you can get to those answers: you can crunch the numbers (quantitative research) or listen to consumers (qualitative research). As we said, it's not easy, you need both—plus the understanding of the important differences between the two.

You don't have to be a billion-dollar brand to do quantitative and qualitative research. It's as simple as asking *everyone* who comes into your store (and keeping all the data for analysis) "how did you hear about us?" (quantitative research) and "what made you stop in?" (qualitative research). It's also now infinitely easier on the Web, where you can track links, trace pages, and stay on top of the way people access your site and shop online.

The essential task is to personalize and humanize your customer. Get to know your prospects as if they're going to be your houseguests. What will they want for supper? What movie should you rent or order for them? What TV channels will they turn to? What's the play list on their iPod? What book should you leave on their night table? What Web sites do they surf? What stores will they want to shop in?

Try something seemingly simple with your team. With the data in hand, have everyone sit down and write a one-page description of your customer. Then gather in a room and compare the descriptions they've written. Are they all saying the same thing? And is it consistent with the data so it's spot on target?

Or take a minute and call in a coworker. Do a one-on-one session in which you both try to write an accurate description of your customer(s). Then think about this: if two employees of the company that makes (or markets or advertises) the product can't agree, how likely is it that the consumer will relate to what you're trying to say?

And that's not all. Interestingly we find that corporations and their suppliers (ad agencies, Web developers, creative resources) don't always view the customer the same way. Clients (read MBAs) love the numbers. They're happiest wading through quantitative research. Agencies better understand qualitative research in search for the nuances the numbers represent.

Time and time again we find the above exercises can't be successfully completed. We usually find lots of close generalities, but the key nuggets of information that separate your brand's customers from your competitors' customers either aren't known, aren't part of the specific vocabulary of your marketing team, or are described in different ways depending on which team member we talk with. Either way, you and your brand are in trouble.

Virtually everything you do nowadays can be catalogued under the once-jargon phrase "micromarketing." Exactness is what is called for in today's marketing, even if you're still working under the mistaken idea that you're a mass marketer. Today's successful advertising appeals on a one-to-one basis. Personalize it. It's the depth of the communication that's critical.

Think about the advertising that appeals to you and how it captures that appeal. It resonates with who you are, what you think, what you feel. In fact, if the message doesn't catch your frame of mind, it doesn't stick. And if it's annoying enough, then you use whatever technology is at your disposal to just zap it by.

Do you hear yourself saying, "Who the hell are they talking to?" Your customers do the same thing. Which is why we say "know your customers."

How do you truly become an expert on your target market? How do you get your team to thoroughly understand that target and the importance of using a common and precise vocabulary to describe that target? The answer is to spend time listening. Here are some ideas to get you started:

1. Get the IT and Research departments to download every bit of customer data they have that describes your category and brand's customer. And have them put it into a form that can be studied.
2. Get out there in the real world and meet people who you think are your customers and prospects. Spend some time at retail or whatever outlets are selling your product or service. If someone buys your brand, ask if you can talk to him awhile. Conduct an instant interview. Do it a few times until you think you'll know the answers before you ask the question. Then do the same thing with people who are passing up your brand for a competitor's. Why do they prefer another brand to yours? What could you do to

make your brand more appealing to them? And if you manage to convince a person to put down the competitor's brand and buy yours instead, think about that persuasion factor. (And consider switching to sales or motivational speaking.)

3. Go on sales calls with the sales team. The further you get from your customers, the greater the chances you'll lose touch with them. Missing trends is one of the easiest ways to lose control of your brand. The smartest way to stay on top is to stay in touch. So no matter what level you've risen to, make sure you hit the sales floor at least once a year.

4. Study the syndicated research that's available for your product category. Broad strokes. Build some hypotheses using your firsthand, face-to-face–gathered information.

5. Use custom research to further the process of listening to the consumer to prove or disprove the hypotheses that you've developed through the above steps. It'll be worth every minute and dollar you spend. And while you're at it, take your ad agency to a retailer. Yes, it's true that most creatives should be left alone in dark spaces. But force them to come up for air now and then. Brilliant advertising is the perfect intersection of the customer, the selling message, and the culture. If the creatives are out of touch

with any of those three, they don't have a prayer at getting the advertising right. So as much as it pains you (and them), include your creative people on these fact-finding missions. Tell them it's a field trip. Creatives like field trips.

If all this sounds like work, you betcha! There's good news and bad news here. The good news is: knowing your customer will enable you to make informed, intelligent, effective decisions. The bad news is: if you don't intimately know your customer, you're gonna be out of a job.

John Wanamaker, founder of Wanamaker's Department Store, was famously quoted as saying "half of my advertising is wasted, I just don't know which half." (In England, they credit Lord Leverhulme—founder of Unilever—with that quote. Being Americans, we prefer Wanamaker. When this book gets published in England we'll give credit to Leverhulme. We're such whores.) Those days are long gone. If you can spend money on it, you can figure some way to measure it. And every client CEO and COO should be eager to demand those measurements. No other area of your company spends the money that marketing and advertising spends with so little measure of results. Learn from the best and most sophisticated manufacturers about how to find a new level of expertise and set goals that can be measured in an almost Six Sigma manner. Marketers and advertisers have long been getting a virtual free ride. Like it or not, methodologies such as Six Sigma are eventually going to be applied to advertising, media, and marketing.

Audiences are more fragmented. Media buys are more expensive. Great advertising is harder to create. Getting noticed in a crowded field is tougher than ever. Younger audiences are more jaded. The more you understand *exactly* who you're talking to, the better your chances of reaching that audience with effective advertising. Everyone on your team needs to be hitting the yellow bull's-eye with every advertising and promotional effort.

Ready! Aim. Fire! (And we don't mean fire your agency.)

2

Live and Die
by the 80/20 Rule

IT'S LIKELY THAT MOST OF YOUR BUSINESS COMES FROM A loyal, relatively small, core audience. If you study the sales, viewership, attendance, or similar form of measurement that's valid for your business, you'll see that nearly 80 percent (or at least two-thirds) of your business comes from approximately 20 percent of your customers. It's a maxim of marketing that endures.

Satisfied customers. Repeat buyers. Heavy viewers. Frequent fliers. Every industry has a term for this core group, but knowing you've got a core of heavy users is just the first step. Who are they and how do you communicate with them? How do they differ from the rest of your audience? What are their purchase habits and how are you tracking their tastes? Hell, are you even tracking their tastes?

Are they "Early Adopters" who are now bored and are looking forward to something new? "Last Ones In" who will now be resistant to change? "True Loyals" who will go down with the ship? "Mainstreamers" who exist in the white-hot core? (They're the ones in the center of the target we wrote about last chapter.) Treat them well. They deserve all the special attention you can give. Many marketers describe the core target audience as units arrayed in a bucket with a hole in the bottom. The job of the marketer and advertiser is to limit the number of units leaking out the bottom while replacing those who disappear with more new customers whom you pour in from the top. However you view them, treat them well.

No matter how loyal your core buyer group is, tastes change and we all grow older. (Except Steve, who continues to behave like an eight-year-old.) And as new people move into your core buyer group they're likely different from the ones who got there first.

What are those differences? Today's thirty-five-year-old is a very different person than a thirty-five-year-old just twenty years ago. Twenty years ago, no self-respecting thirty-five-year-old would be caught dead driving a Cadillac. Today, an Escalade with bling is the way to go.

And what if people aren't moving into your core customer's narrowly defined demographic segment fast enough? What does that tell you about your business? Should you look for a new core customer segment or look to reinvent your product? Hint: You can't answer that question unless you truly understand why your core audience is what it is.

Talk to people who you think are at the oldest edge of your core customer group. Ask them questions about a broad range of cultural happenings and then ask them about the attributes they apply to your brand. Then do the same to that youngest edge core customer group. People who market to younger audiences see this change phenomenon on an annual basis: when it comes to talking to kids, three to five years defines a separate generational attitude. It isn't until consumers reach their twenties that the attitudinal gaps start to close, but they rarely fully close.

The first people to spot taste trends should be your creative team. They're the ones that should be most active in sampling our culture. The best are exceptionally sensitive to what's hot and what's not. The tricky part is to pay attention to what your creative people are telling you—but don't let them wag the dog. The tastes of New York– and Los Angeles–based creatives are going to be years ahead of the bulk of your audience. Unless your audience is whacko urban twentysomethings. In which case, your New York– and Los Angeles–based creatives are going to only be about six months behind the curve.

A corollary to the 80/20 rule is that it's easier to get increased business from the perimeters of your existing business (infrequent customers, occasional viewers) than it is to develop new business from scratch. That's where line extensions are valuable. Core users and occasional users of Fatso Potato Chips are going to be the first to try Fatso Onion Chips. But before you start diluting your brand, make sure you've got "brand permission" from your core buyer group. Fans of Fatso Potato Chips may not be in a rush to try Fatso Lite Chips.

What does all this mean? Build off of your best customers

and the ones closest to them. Loyalty programs. Clubs. Frequent Flyer Miles. Special offers. Those are just a few of the ways you can reach out to your core buyer group and reward their loyalty. Then work out from the core to bring in new audiences. It's a lot easier to make a sale to someone who's already interested in what you've got to say.

And if you're nodding in agreement, we've just proven our point.

3

Read What Your Customer
Reads, Watch What She Watches

IMAGINE YOU SPEND YOUR DAYS DEVELOPING OVER-THE-counter medical ads and marketing plans for aging Baby Boomers. If so, the last thing you probably want to do at home is turn on the TV and watch reruns of *Columbo.*

Do it. Not every day, but at least once a week. You need to tap into your customer's media habits. It's another way to understand her, build a relationship with her, and sell her.

One of the advantages of watching and reading your customer's media is you get to see your ads—and your competitors'. You'll come across your own advertising in context. Did it surprise you? Did it stand out from all the other ads for the same product trying to reach the same audience? Did the magazine bury you in the back? Did the TV network sandwich your ad between two competitors? Note your first reactions to seeing your own ads. And if you didn't see your own ads, that should tell you something, too!

In one form or another, we'll say this time and again in this book: Successfully communicating to the consumer requires knowing the consumer. The closer you get to the consumer the more successful your selling will be. People buy from friends. From people they like. People buy from people they perceive are like them. The more you get into the head of the target audience, the more you'll be able to talk to them in their own language (Tip #37).

One of the best ways to understand your potential customer is to read the magazines he reads and watch the TV programs and movies he watches. Media outlets (TV, radio, magazines, newspapers, Web sites) live and die by knowing what their target audience is interested in. They've already gotten the customer to buy what they're selling—get on their coattails!

Steve tries to read at least one issue of every magazine on the newsstands each year aimed at key demographics (especially those who are client customers). It keeps him abreast of what the consumer is thinking and what big issues are grabbing the national media and helping to set the cultural agenda.

And before starting an assignment we read every magazine the user of the product or service is likely to read, particularly the magazines we're going to be advertising in. We also hunt for blogs that cover both the client's products and the competitors'. In the wild frontier of the Internet, one angry consumer or disgruntled former employee can do a lot more damage than in the past. We want to know what the consumer is thinking. We want to know what the influentials are thinking. We want to know how other companies who are seeking their share of her spending are selling her.

Most important, we want to know what's on consumer minds and how they express themselves. Don't just look at the pictures. Read the letters to the editor. The regular columns. And most of all, read the ads.

Your company doesn't operate in a vacuum and your advertising doesn't run in a vacuum. Be a media hound—it's the only way to stay current with your consumer. Pull together an informal lunch with the brand guys and the creative team and have each try to stump the other with names and concepts from the world of entertainment, sports, business news. You'll be shocked at how little each group knows about what's seemingly important in the life of the other. Pick up the annual issue of *People* magazine's "25 Most Important People." If you don't know who all twenty-five are, you've lost touch with the consumer.

Did your grandmother care who Bobbie Darin was? Do your kids even know the name? Do you listen to Linkin Park? Is Allen Iverson growing up? What's the longest running story in the tabloids? News, celebrity, and pop culture live in a narrow age range, usually reported by the media. Advertising doesn't wag the dog, but it's got to know which way the nose is pointing.

4

Know Your Brand Image

QUIZ: WHAT'S THE DIFFERENCE BETWEEN YOUR BRAND AND your brand image? Answer: Everything. A brand is just a name. Its image is its importance in the mind of the consumer. Call it Branding. Brand Image. Brand Essence. Brand Personality. Brand Promise. Brand Permission. It's all the same thing. What your brand stands for in the mind of the consumer is as important as—or in many cases more important than—what you make or do.

In real estate, it's location, location, location. In marketing it's brand, brand, brand. Everyone talks about it. There's no shortage of consultants who'll charge you huge sums of money to advise you on it. And most of us take it too much for granted. It's not just a name, it's the collective experience people have had with your product or service. Start diluting it and you'll wake up one day with a name that means . . . nothing. Tamper with your brand at your own risk.

It's the single most important item management must manage. (Even more important in our minds than finances because it's the brand that generates the revenues.) It's not something you can hold in your hand, it's not tangible, it's not permanent, it's subject to emotion. Yet it's the sum total of what you make, do, sell, service, or show to the world. Mess with it at your own risk. Because even the best manager of cash will run out of cash without a great brand delivering more cash on daily basis. Yes, a great brand, managed brilliantly is an annuity. Get the picture? BRAND IS ALL!

What are the basic brand image building blocks? They're the promises of the brand's benefits that consumers either instinctively attach to the brand or are taught to attach to the brand.

What those promises should be, how to communicate those promises, and how to keep those promises fresh and relevant are the great stuff of marketing and advertising. Take the Volkswagen ad we mentioned in Tip #1: Many years ago, to attract a younger audience, Oldsmobile tried the campaign "This is not your father's Oldsmobile," alienating both the younger audience and loyal Oldsmobile fans. What if Volkswagen had done "This is not your mother's Volkswagen"? It's the same campaign, but "This is not your father's Oldsmobile" was a line probably thought up by an account executive. The creative team never turned the concept into a magical campaign. Volkswagen had exactly the same problem, but they gave the creatives room to come up with an execution that gave people the *experience* that "this is not your father's Volkswagen."

Brand image is critical knowledge. It's gotta be measured and remeasured and you've got to manage from that measurement. (You can't manage what you don't measure—you'll read that again and again in this book.)

Learn how to sell your brand from your brand image's strength and learn how to continually manage that strength to coincide with consumer sentiment and behavior. While you can push, nudge, and point in the right direction, ultimately the consumer will lead you, not vice versa.

Your product must deliver, reinforce, and never disappoint the image that it has with its best customers and prospects. And it must stay in step with consumer thinking, if not a bit ahead of it, to keep sales on a continually upward-sloping curve.

Does the above sound preachy? Well, it should. Those who preach the gospel of brand are the ones who succeed in the long term. Our memory boxes are filled with meetings we've had or heard about where the importance of brand image has been dismissed because of some type of short-term crisis.

Here are three lists of brands. One for great brands, another for once great brand names, and a third for those undergoing change. Each is probably reasonably pertinent to your life. Can you pinpoint what each stands for?

GREAT	ONCE GREAT	UNDERGOING CHANGE
Apple	Avon	AOL
Bloomingdale's	Compaq	Cadillac
BMW	Gap	E*Trade
Crest	Kodak	IBM
Pepsi	Sears	Macy's
Yahoo	Vioxx	Motorola

Two mentions from brands noted above:

Year after year, Sears management was told it was losing touch with its customers. Jeff was in meeting after meeting in the Sears board room when the Ogilvy team walked out almost in tears, because their understanding of why the Sears brand was losing its appeal fell upon deaf ears.

Motorola heeded the brand brilliance of the late Geoffrey Frost to grab hold of and adopt the immediate culture of their most profitable customers. The result: higher sales and the beginnings of a hot brand image.

Without knowing what your brand stands for in the mind of the consumer, today's sales figures mean nothing. Zip. Nada. Sales may go up. Sales may go down. Bean counters can tell you to the microunit exactly how many widgets you've sold this month, last month, and maybe even project for next month. But unless you, as a manager and marketer, understand *why* people are buying (or not buying) your product, you have no control over the future sales curve of the product. Sure, you can have clearance sales. You can have seasonal promotions. You can offer rebates. All those will move product off the shelves. But without understanding what your brand means, you really are managing in the dark.

The key reason for continuing to conduct research is to understand the market and your brand's place and strength in it. Start with your own sales team. Listen to them. They have their finger on the pulse of the market on an everyday basis. Filter out their daily frustrations and you have a second powerful understanding of just where your brand stands in relation to its competitors. Talking to your sales force is the simplest, cheapest form of brand research you can do.

Changing a brand image is one of the toughest tasks in marketing. And in many cases it just isn't possible to successfully make that change. Somewhere along the line, American business stopped using the word "no." But it's a very effective word. It acknowledges that some things can't be done: some assignments can't be achieved, some deadlines can't be met. The bookshelves are filled with books that attempt to turn no into yes, but they're probably a waste of everyone's time. While we believe all the tips in this book can make a difference in your life, we won't lie to you about things we think can't be accomplished. No is no. No bull.

What about line extensions? Can they refresh a brand and keep it alive? Yes and no. On the positive side they can keep the brand fresh, enhance its shelf space to help keep awareness high, make the competitor brands look tired and old, and bring in new buyers who bring a new and fresh energy to the brand. So Crest can come out with Tartar Control and Extra Whitening and every variation in between. What used to be advertising promises are now the brand extensions themselves.

On the other hand they can hurt brand image: if the line extension is downscale it can lower the perceived value of the brand; too upscale and it can appear to put the brand out of the reach of its loyal buyers; not consistent with the brand's image (e.g., a Nike bandage); or a copycat version of a competitor and not up to the perceived standards of the brand. Successful line extension needs "brand permission." And either you've got it or you don't. Nike can make clothes. Coca-Cola can't. (For those of you who don't remember that debacle, around 1980, Coca-Cola actually licensed a line of clothes and opened retail stores around the country. For five minutes.)

So what are we telling you? Brand image is critical, measurable, and manageable. But because it's intangible and subject to the emotions of the consumer and management, it takes a team of professionals to handle brand image well.

Most important? Anything can be branded. If you're thinking "my product is generic, it can't be branded," think again. Whether it was Chris Moseley's brilliant job of branding Discovery Channel (a cable network? How do you brand a cable network?), Ed McCabe's job of branding Perdue Chicken, Christos Cotsakos's job of branding online brokerage, the biggest mistake you can make is thinking you can't build a brand. Any product, service, feature, or benefit can be turned into a brand with the right marketing.

What's the value of a great brand image? There are a number of consulting firms, in business for years, that quantify brand image in dollars and cents for both management and the Wall Street analysts who track those companies.

The monetization of brand value enables those who manage the company to actually think about their brands as assets on the balance sheet. That tangible perspective often helps managers not used to participating in the marketing wars. Thought about in those terms, marketing and advertising isn't an expense, it's an equity-building division with a quantifiable ROI. And that's the demanding future that marketing and advertising are facing.

So roll up your sleeves, get down to the sales floor, and start understanding what your brand means. Then read what we've got to say about the value and purpose of research. And the next time your investors want to know why your sales are up (or down), you'll actually be able to tell them—from the consumer's point of view!

5

Be an Expert on the Benefits of Your Product or Service

A PACKAGED GOODS COMPANY IS LAUNCHING BRAND EXTENsions of their peanut butter: Peanut Butter and Jelly, Peanut Butter and Marshmallow, Peanut Butter and Jam, Peanut Butter and Crisped Rice.

Peanut Butter and Jelly—sounds yummy. Sounds like a natural. Peanut Butter and Jam—well, sure (if you're doing Jelly you should do Jam). Peanut Butter and Marshmallow—um, gulp. Okay, if you like that sort of thing. Peanut Butter and Crisped Rice—you're kidding? Who would want to try a jar of Peanut Butter and Crisped Rice?

Sadly, Steve was just a junior copywriter at the time and he thought the Crisped Rice one was a loser . . . and never even tried the product before writing the commercial.

You know where this is going. And by the way, Steve finally tried the (successful) Peanut Butter and Crisped Rice (on his next job). It was delicious.

Even if you don't like the product, there's a reason the company makes it and there's a reason people buy it. Those are two different reasons. As a marketer and advertising executive, you've got to be an expert on the second reason—but also understand the first.

Start with the first reason: the reason the company makes it. Find out, as innocently and with as open a mind as possible, why the company makes the product. Even if it's a product that's been around for a hundred years. You'll get a wealth of information from the manufacturer and you'll also uncover a hidden gem or two in how to talk to consumers. Then get to work on reason two: the reason the consumer buys it.

Time and again, Steve would attend commercial auditions and the actors would show up dressed for the part—without having tried the product. ("I'm not a doctor but I'm hoping to play one on TV for a lot of money.") It's a question we always ask at auditions and interviews: "Have you tried our product? What was your experience?" There's an old saying in acting: "Sincerity is the hardest emotion: once you can fake that, you can fake all of them." Actually trying (and believing in) your product is the sincere basis of everything you do. If you don't believe in your company and its products, get another job.

The first step in this part of your job is to use the product. Use it as directed. Use it in myriad other ways. Experiment. If you can't use it (e.g., denture glue), ask someone who can use it to help you do your job. Delve into being the heaviest user the product ever had. Then you'll be ready to ask the questions you need to begin the selling process.

What are the benefits of the product to the consumer? What is it about your product or service that makes someone go out and specifically ask for your brand by name? Is it quality? Is it value? Is it the patented thingamajig? Does it make their life easier? Is it more convenient? Is it status? Do they use it in ways you never intended? Will it walk their dog and wash their windows for them?

Arm & Hammer makes baking soda. They made it for baking, but consumers had dozens of other uses. When A&H learned about the box in the refrigerator, they started promoting its use to a wider audience, redesigned the box for that use, and revitalized the sales of their brand. How many people are putting your product to uses that you don't know about and that could revitalize your sales?

Knowing why people buy or use what you do is especially important if you market an upscale product or service.

With everyday products, it's (often) obvious. The benefit to the consumer is fairly clear. But even then, you can be fooled, so take the time to find out from consumers what they perceive as the product's key benefits. With upscale products or services, it's often less obvious what the benefit to the consumer is. But if you find the key benefits or benefit, you'll find the catalyst for marketeing your service in a way no competitor can use.

Even if it's a service that's been around for forty years, it's important to know what the key benefit to the consumer is from the consumer's perspective. Once upon a time, someone had a good idea. They would provide a service to consumers or other business people that they really needed. They built a company by appealing to that need. Over time, chances are you (and the consumer) have taken that need for granted. If your research is able to go back to that blank page and imagine you've just invented this service for the first time, you'll likely rediscover that basic need.

Find that basic consumer need and use it to build interest and attention. If you're selling something people want, you've already made 70 percent of the sale. The other 30 percent? Well, that's what you and your ad agency are for. Just make sure you know what it is you're selling—and why!

Over the years, there've been a lot of so-called rules about what marketing can and cannot do. Whole categories of consumer goods and services were never advertised or promoted, because manufacturers and marketers accepted the conventional wisdom that there were generics. About thirty years ago, a chicken farmer from Maryland came up to New York City looking for an ad agency to brand his chickens. Many agencies simply dismissed the idea that you could brand a commodity like chicken. Scali, McCabe & Sloves was smart enough to share Frank Perdue's vision. That should be a lesson to everyone who's ever thought, "We can't build this product into a brand."

The other side of the coin is a benefit you can't promote. Sometimes consumers find uses for products that the company—secretly grateful for the sales—wishes they didn't know about. Steve went skiing once with the international brand manager for Preparation H. At the top of the run, the brand manager offered Steve a tube. Puzzled, he watched as Axel, the brand manager, used it as a lip balm to prevent wind chafing. Gee—thanks but no thanks.

6

Do You Know the Brand History?

WHERE'S YOUR BRAND BEEN? WHAT'S WORKED? WHAT'S FAILED? Do you and everyone who works with you know the history of your brand?

We've long been amazed at the level of mushroom management when it comes to brand history. (Mushroom management, for those of you who don't know, is an executive strategy: "Keep your employees in the dark and feed 'em shit.") Don't let it happen to you. Question, question, question. Dig deep. Demand a historical context for what you are going to do. Remember that those who don't know and learn from history are doomed to repeat it. Clearly you don't want to make mistakes, never mind mistakes that have been made before. Two examples to make the point:

Brand history takes many forms. What about last year's sales convention? What worked? What didn't? When do you start planning next year's? We work with broadcast and cable television networks, and every year they act as if the fall premiere and upfront sales presentations are a complete surprise. Any annual event within marketing's scope should be reviewed and analyzed immediately after the event—and then a twelve-month timeline should be put in place for the next one.

Package goods ad agencies used to be masters of this tip. On the second day a new employee went to work, the account team would show up at the person's office to welcome them to the ad agency and then spend hours with a stack of commercials and print ads to bring the person completely up to speed on the history of the brand: when it was launched, early successes and failures, evolution of the brand, consumer acceptance, spin-offs, variations (Original, Lite, Low-Carb, Extra, Crunchy, you name it). Even if you were only assigned to one portion of the brand, a good account team would take you through a solid briefing so you clearly understood the entire history of the brand, right up to the current market situation and the need you had to fulfill.

Bad account teams would be dismissive if you asked about strategies. Good account teams would explain strategies that had been thought about and rejected or tested and failed. Or, never thought of and "thanks for that idea." At the end of the session, you felt you knew as much about the history of the brand as anyone working on the business.

It's a lost art, although brand is the company's single greatest asset. Go figure.

No, don't go figure! Make it happen at your company. Create a way to learn your brand's history. If there's no system in place for keeping an ongoing library of all marketing materials—advertising, commercials, brochures, collateral, point-of-purchase, co-op dealer ads, every type of communication—start one now as you scrounge up as many old materials as possible.

Start it today. If you're lucky enough to have a junior staff or an intern working for you, put one of them on the case and see if you can round up from your ad agencies, media agencies, creative resource group, in-house agency and employees at least one copy of every campaign and all the research.

Someone's got to do the grunt work. Making the intern gather your marketing materials will be a crash course in teaching him or her about marketing (make sure you review the materials with him and explain the history of the brand; it'll be a good education for both of you). But when the material's gathered, make sure you're the person in charge, not the intern. Being the Knowledge Officer who is the expert on the brand and the competition is no job for an intern; it's a job for a VP—or someone who hopes to be a VP real soon!

Even if you have to settle for black-and-white photocopies and order your commercials from a screening service, try to round up a sample of everything. The next call is to work with IT to get everything on your company's Intranet. With the advent of immense storage technologies and Intranets there's no excuse for not having every bit of brand information right at hand.

Next meet with a team of the top go-getters that you want to work with.

Do it over a long lunch.

Don't position it as a "learning" session; keep it light and low-key. ("I thought it'd help us all to take a look at how far we've come and how we can move ahead faster and meet or exceed our objectives.")

Then work as a team with an objective point of view—no editorializing, preaching, or denigration of any of the work. Just run through all of it. Concentrate on specific campaigns that solved problems at the time. And if the campaign failed, recognize it with no attribution of blame. (Sad to say most times you will find no measurement on the success or failure of a campaign. Don't perpetuate that behavior. Measure so you can manage.)

As you're going through it, take a look around and notice the "ah-hah's" going off in everyone's mind as they start to understand, often for the first time, why your brand is what it is.

Make sure everyone is listening to the discussions. Keep it light. And make sure from that point forward, you've got an up-to-date library of work and an established methodology for welcoming new employees onto the team.

PS: The keeper of the flame is a critical job that should be highly rewarded in terms of career advancement. You'll observe how many other senior people from other divisions come to whoever that keeper is (it should be you) and send their employees to be briefed.

PPS: Consider putting the best stuff up on your Internet site or blog. It makes for fascinating viewing by fans and students of marketing. Some "antique" commercials will make your site more interesting. It shows you have a sense of brand history. It will make your site "stickier" and increase hits.

7

Does Everyone Know the Competitive History?

TAKE EVERYTHING YOU'VE JUST READ IN TIP #6. DO THE SAME thing for your competitor's advertising.

Sports teams spend millions of dollars scouting out the competition (they even scout in Little League), learning their every move. Why? Because it works. When the game is on the line they know that competitive knowledge can be the difference between winning and losing.

How well do you know your competitors' history? How often do you think about what their next move is going to be?

Far too little time is spent analyzing the history of category advertising. Far too little thought goes into outsmarting competitors whose customers buy similarly positioned brands.

We're surprised at how little reaction there is to competitive activities. If you're supposed to be working fast these days, you should also be nimble. If the competition's running an ad that could be taking business away from you, how do you respond? At the very least, do you take the time to analyze the competition's advertising? Do you really think what your competitor does has no effect on your brand? Do you really think that he might not know something about communicating to your mutual customers? Do you really think there's nothing he does that you should analyze and insert into your own strategic and tactical thinking?

Big companies like Coke know who their competitors are. Pepsi? Guess again. It's not only Pepsi, it's not just other carbonated beverages, it's virtually all fluids. When someone reaches for a glass of water, Coca Cola wants a share of that market. They seek not only share of market but also share of thirst.

One of the biggest categories where competitive issues don't seem to concern our clients is, amazingly, cable TV networks. Time and time again we give seminars to networks and ask our audience of marketers and promotion people to talk with us about who they are selling against and what programs competitors are running in key time slots—almost always we get blank stares.

"Were we supposed to know that?" they ask.

"Only if you want to successfully promote against your competitors and get the viewer to watch your program versus his," we respond. That gets worried nods.

But there's little we can do about it if network leaders don't take promoting select time slots and select programs seriously in terms of the consumer having a choice. Choice? Hell, the consumer has an average of 100 choices every minute in the average cable household, never mind all the other media, DVRs, and other leisure-time activities.

Long ago, every brand manager developed a comprehensive competitive book and could tell you virtually everything there was to know about his competitors' marketing activities. We understand that there's no time for that today and that change comes all too fast, but marketing efforts and advertising don't run in a competitive vacuum and no advertising should be developed in a vacuum.

There's too much money being spent and wasted in advertising today not to give more thought to what is going on, why it's going on, and what brands are benefiting the most from those activities.

So take time to study your competitor's marketing. Study his promotions. Study his advertising. Learn from them. David Ogilvy once said, "The consumer is not a moron, she's your wife." Let us add to that, "Your competitor isn't a moron, he's at least as smart as you are and he's planning to beat your brains out."

Will you let him?

WHAT'S YOUR OBJECTIVE?

*"For some reason, we aren't appealing enough to those
awful little bastards everyone hates."*

A copywriter we know used to have a sign on her wall: When shooting rapids in a canoe, if you say 'I don't know,' the river will decide for you. In marketing if you don't know what to do, the river of consumerism will drop your brand right over the falls.

You and your team need to have a clear and detailed plan of where you're going and how you expect to get there. And equally important, that plan needs to be actively managed by the team, with changes and alterations as the consumer landscape data is refined into information and analyzed into knowledge.

Climb into your canoe—and get ready to ride the rapids.

8

Know Where You Want to Take the Brand

ALICE IN WONDERLAND IS LOST IN THE WOODS. SHE COMES TO a fork in the road and the Cheshire Cat appears in a tree.

"I'm lost," Alice wails.

"Where do you want to go?" the Cheshire Cat asks.

"I don't know," Alice responds.

"Then any road will take you there."

Do you know where you want to take your brand? Does anyone in your company know? And if there is someone who knows, why are they keeping it a secret?

At many companies, there isn't a clear, precise objective. Or worse: the objective that's formalized is such a stretch that it could never be met in the defined timeframe or budget.

Not knowing where you want to take your company/brand—realistically—is management malpractice at its worst. It's a virtual guarantee for financial failure.

Setting realistic goals. Regular (and frequent) measurement of process. (Uh-oh. There's that measurement thing again.) Those are the first must-do steps in the building of great brands (and careers).

How should you set those goals? With a two-day off-site session. Can't round everyone up or don't have the time? If you believe that, it won't be long before you won't have a job, either. Remember, the brand will likely outlast the careers of everyone at the meeting and possible even the company. Your careers depend on brand building.

Here's a well-defined list of process steps on how to set realistic goals in one major brand objectives meeting. (You may want to do a variation of the following, but our suggestion is that you don't vary it too much.)

1. Start with a two-day retreat with key senior managers; but also include the smartest and most valuable junior managers in the company. Make sure the heads of sales, research, and marketing, and your creative director and/or head of advertising are there, too.

   If you're brave enough to invite an important customer into the meeting and it can be done to strengthen that relationship rather than undermine it, then give it a shot. If it makes sense, invite your design company CEO or your outsourced manufacturing company CEO in addition to your agency's creative director into the meeting. They'll have valuable outsider perspective. They'll also be able to hear where you're planning to go and can stay ahead of the curve. Just be sure they're prepared and you're not compromising your position with them or theirs with you.

2. Keep the spreadsheet programs off in Day One! Steve remembers when personal computers first came into the business world. His boss was fiddling with Lotus 1,2,3 on an early Apple. Curious, Steve asked what that was. His boss gave a succinct answer: "It's a weapon—upwards. Ain't nobody going to argue with a bunch of numbers generated by a computer."

   Keep your hands off the keyboard. Spreadsheets spread lies when they're the first step. They manage numbers not brands. They're management-thinking not customer-thinking, and they rarely reflect the competitive and realistic marketplace. They usually reflect what the spreadsheet jockey thinks management wants to see and what they will buy. But it's the end user's (customer's) buy that is most important to the company. (Then again, if you need to save your job for the short term, by all means crank up the laptops.)

3. Be prepared to listen, and make sure everyone else learns to listen. Be prepared to challenge, and make sure everyone else learns how to challenge—without getting personal. (By the way, if you can't stand the thought of going away with those people for two days, that tells you something right there.)

4. Hire an objective third party to facilitate the discussion. No input is required from that third party ex-

cept to keep the meeting on track and on time and to prevent any one view from dominating during the initial presentations. And it's our experience that with a third party running the meeting, participants become more honest and less defensive as they see the bosses around the table doing the same hard work.

5. Put together an agenda exploring where the company or brand has been and where those drivers of it think it can be taken. This is the brand-map. Competitive brands must also be shown on the brand-map. Keep it clear, keep it fact-based.

6. Let every attendee start with the elevator presentation. Steve believes that if you can't explain your job to your five-year-old, you're in trouble. More important: can you pitch your company to a potential investor on an elevator from the first to the fifteenth floor? If not, you ain't getting the money. So give every attendee a chance to make the elevator presentation and then another forty-five minutes to lay out the long-term vision. While forty-five minutes seems tight, we've seen comprehensive presentations made in twenty. We prefer the twenty-minute format (plus ten for Q&A), but we're feeling magnanimous as of this writing. That presentation should clearly delineate what they know, what they think they know, what they think, what they believe, and

where they think things can be improved. That's a lot to pack into an hour's presentation, so it's essential that everyone be totally prepared.

7. There'll be lots of duplication at the meeting. Boredom and fatigue can easily set in. Plan on frequent breaks to keep people in focus and not worrying about things they've left undone at the office. (Cell phones turned off during the meetings.) Everyone needs to listen for the nuances that will make a big difference or the breakthrough idea that will make a huge difference. They can only do it if they're fresh and focused. Twenty minutes of discussion time should be available after each presentation. Clear, cogent nonpolitical, not-personalized discussion. (It's the moderator's job to keep that discussion on track and not personal.)

8. At the end of the initial presentations top management should select what it thinks are the best, most realistic objectives, ideas, and rationale(s) and present them for further discussion.

That should take you through the end of Day One. Day Two should start with a quick recap by the moderator and then turn into a blueprint building session for the future.

9. After the brand objectives are defined come the most critical steps. Now is the time to determine "what it

will take to win." Do you need to increase your ad budget? Do you need to redesign the product? Nothing should be sacred—the future of the brand (and your job) is at stake. Don't let this meeting turn into a Monday morning quarterbacking session. Anyone can talk about what's wrong.

A former number two of a GE division passed this step along to us. He's convinced that this crucial analysis and then "the action steps that put the win in play" are what make the difference between great brands and also-rans.

10. Follow the "what will it take to win" discussion with an outline of specific action steps everyone can begin to take to solidify the individual goals they'll need for the brand to win.

11. Only then should spreadsheets begin to be developed to formalize the plan into measurable criteria. Every mile along the recommended route must be put into some type of metric against which those responsible can manage their everyday jobs.

The meeting isn't meant to let management escape its responsibility. It's to make sure that management fulfills its responsibility to listen to all the key players in the company.

Here's another tip from another client. They had regular sessions they called "the foxhole." Senior management (including the chairman and CEO) picked eight employees at random from different departments of the company and they gathered in a room for an afternoon. Anything could be said. It was a chance for the mailroom guy to really tell the president everything that the employee felt was wrong. Invariably, the president would make the employee clean up the mess. Right there. Even if it meant making phone calls from the conference room and calling in outsider vendors or other department heads. There's a reason for the expression "there are no atheists in foxholes."

Time and time again (especially over the last few months) we've heard, "Management doesn't listen. They just go their own way and the marketing and advertising aren't geared to help fulfill management's goals."

There's just no excuse for that. And now that you have the meeting blueprint, go for it!

9

Map a Clear Route of How You'll Take Your Brand to the Destination

DO YOU HAVE A CLEAR ROAD MAPPED OUT FOR YOUR ADVER-
tising? Or are you just using the brown wall approach? (That's
where you throw a lot of shit at the wall and hope some of it
sticks.)

From time-to-time Eastern mysticism, ancient texts, and
shamanistic practices become popular in the business community. (Musashi. Sun Tzu's *The Art of War.* Werner Erhard.)
We think they show up when the brown wall approach has
failed and people are wondering what to do next. The only
truly useful programs we've ever heard of from the "mysteri-
ous East" are the long-range plans of companies like Toyota
and Matsushita. These companies have corporate plans that
extend five, ten, fifty, and one hundred years into the future.
Yes, they review and update them, but at least they know
where they're hoping to go.

Take a look at your advertising and marketing plan. Not
the budget, the plan. And not the media plan, either. We're
talking about a written plan that says (in effect), "We're going
to do X in order to achieve Y and this is how we'll do it within
Z time frame." Is it even written? With documentation? Have
you shared it with your boss and your employees? Do they
agree with it and support it?

We're not talking about the PowerPoint presentation that tactically lays out the fourth quarter promotion; we're not talking about the media plan that tactically lays out how you're going to put your message in front of your audience. We're talking about the plan that specifies your efforts for your brand over the next twelve to sixty months—and beyond. (There's no reason to do spreadsheets beyond three years. Everything, and we mean everything, beyond that time frame is a wild-ass guess.)

If you're a worker bee, go (gently) into your boss's office and ask if you can review the brand/marketing plan for the next few years. Don't be surprised if he hasn't got it written down. (If you want to move up from worker bee to queen bee, when your boss admits there isn't a written plan, volunteer to write it. In a matter of months you'll become the most indispensable employee in the marketing group.)

What does it look like? Hint: We hope it's less than two pages. Yes, you might want to attach some Excel spreadsheets behind it for support (or as a weapon), but you should be able to clearly and simply lay out what your plans are, where you're going, and how you plan to get there.

What that plan is will depend on your business, your product, your service, and what stage of the business cycle your company is in. Are you a blue chip? A start-up? Web-based? Global? It's going to be different for each company, but the good ones will all have one thing in common: a method of measuring results. (M'gosh! That measurement thing again!)

We established Unconventional Wisdom in 1987. Just in time for the stock market crash and the subsequent recession. From 1987 to 1991 we would sit in partner meetings staring at the five-year plan we'd made up before opening the company and asking ourselves, "Where was this recession in our plan?" We would try to blame each other for not including the recession in our business plan. But after we had a good laugh, we'd turn back to the plan, incorporate the reality of the situation (the plan is a working document), and get to work on building the business.

The plan isn't some secret document. Yes, you should have security procedures in place, NDAs, and non-compete agreements. You should make sure Human Resources has properly vetted your employees and put in place an enforceable security system. But you've got to trust the people you've hired and you've got to make them part of the process of reaching your goals.

Steve once went on a job interview for a position he wasn't particularly interested in. Over dinner, his prospective employer asked Steve what he thought his job would be. He started describing how he would assess the staff, evaluate the resources, review the budget, blah, blah, blah. After letting him ramble on, the interviewer stopped the conversation: "Your job is to make me look good," the perspective employer said. "My job is to see you get the credit for it." P.S.: Steve took the job over dinner and worked tirelessly for that man!

From the tactical advertising point of view the following should be done (and while you're at it, you should apply this thinking to the many other tactical areas of marketing):

1. Know and make sure your team knows the objectives toward which you are all working.
2. Establish firm benchmarks against which advertising success will be measured. These can be awareness measures, attitudinal measures, or communication measures. Whatever you select, make sure that the research can accurately measure progress toward the selected goal. And don't change the measure or the system of measurement midstream. Consistency in measurement is critical.
3. Clearly establish with your advertising agency (outside or in-house) or staff how you're going to measure their performance.
4. Agree with your agency how you're going to resolve issues if they don't meet their performance goals.
5. Establish how you're going to hold your product brand group's feet to the fire.

Share the map with everyone, make sure everyone's heading in the same direction, and then go for your goals.

10

Quality Is the Absence of Non-Quality Signals

HUH?

Think about it. Quality is the absence of non-quality signals.

It's a critical point of view Jeff has long borrowed from a fellow named Gene Casey, who was a first-rate product designer. Jeff wasn't sure about the line when he first heard it; he thought it was a bit of design jargon. Steve, too, had no idea what the phrase meant when Jeff first mentioned it to him. Now Steve agrees that it's a basic insight into successful marketing. It isn't jargon, it's brilliant thinking. In fact, Malcolm Gladwell's book *Blink* is entirely about this subject.

How many times have you tried to define quality and come up short? Try these: Ever get a resume with a misspelling (a non-quality signal)? You immediately toss it in the garbage. Ever sit in a luxury car, frowned, and questioned the look and feel of the dashboard (a subconscious non-quality signal)? You think "not very smart of them, probably not worth the money." Quality is, indeed, the absence of non-quality signals.

How often do you find yourself lost in a company's phone tree—and then hanging up without buying the item you were after? That's another non-quality signal.

Consumers do the same thing to your advertising and marketing all the time. Too difficult to navigate your Web site? Not easy to obtain the information they want? Too difficult to go through the order process? They're gone, and so is the sale.

Your commercial too boring to sit through? Your advertisement too jargon-ridden to read?

Put in that context, clarifying your marketing becomes an easy process. Just go through it all and remove all the non-quality signals.

1. Review all your marketing operations as an outsider. Search for the things that would annoy you if you were a prospect or a buyer.
2. Use your family and friends to back you up if you're a small company. Use a professional researcher or consultant if you can afford it.
3. Ask your sales people about their experiences with your marketing materials.

Make sure everyone is honest with you, don't be defensive, and fix what's wrong. Thank you Gene Casey, wherever you are. And we hope we eliminated all the non-quality signals in this book.

WHERE DO YOU WANT TO GO?

W here do you want to go? The answer's simple: you want to go where your best customers are and where they're headed. Ideally, you want to get there a little bit before them. Research provides the best opportunity to understand where that is.

But caution flags are necessary. Research needs to be conducted honestly and consistently, and it needs to be listened to even if the results aren't what you or management would like them to be.

Research is critical to monitoring and tracking your progress and your brand's progress (or lack thereof). And it's worth a whole section by itself.

11

Do Quantitative Research

QUANTITATIVE RESEARCH SHOULD BE ONE OF THE INVIOLATE marketing budget items year after year. There's no substitute for the knowledge to be gained.

Sure it's expensive; sure it's time-consuming. But the only way to really know for sure what consumers are thinking, especially on a trend basis, is to do quantitative research. It's really the only way to keep up with your customers and prospects and be as certain as possible that you're moving in the direction of fulfilling their needs and desires.

Yes, you might be able to get away with quantitative research on an every-other-year basis; but be sure that you don't fall into the trap of doing it on a one-time learning basis. That's a colossal waste of time and money because you just won't have the necessary benchmarks from which to measure changes.

You can't manage what you don't measure (POV #3). And without benchmarks and trend analysis, you have no idea of the direction of consumer thought and (therefore) the direction you need to take your company and your brand's marketing.

What's the ultimate power base of quantitative research?

No less than the lifetime value of your brand. And while the bricks and mortar of any company can be replaced, the value of the brand can't be. It's the single most valuable asset the company possesses, even more important than its employees or stockholders.

Are you getting this? This is one of the sneakily important facts that often get overlooked in the day-to-day hassle with budgets, sales, stock price, etc. It's one of the key points we're going to repeat in capital letters for you speed-readers: THE VALUE OF A BRAND CANNOT BE OVERESTIMATED!

Nothing is better than quantitative research for keeping your brand in step with the consumer and helping you spot the trends.

Trends will tell you of shifts in the mind-sets of consumers, shifts in the perception of your brand, shifts in the perceptions of your competitors' brands. Trends will also tell you whether your advertising is working to the full extent of the time, effort, and money you're spending to support it.

We find most companies are now caught in the middle. Management doesn't want to spend the money. Brand managers don't want to be criticized by anyone. No one wants to be proven wrong about a personal opinion. On the other hand, everyone knows they can't do without research of some kind so they cheat and buy cheap, fast, inconsistent and easy to muzz-around research.

("Muzz?" you ask. "What's muzz?" *Muzz* is Jeff's term for

all those foggy, imprecise, unclear directions that permeate today's marketing world.)

Money is no longer an excuse. You can get great quantitative research straight from companies that use the Web. The results are accurate and it's both faster and cheaper than old-fashioned, twentieth-century ways.

Buyer beware. CEOs beware. Don't drive blind or you'll drive off a cliff. Spend the time to explore how to do your research effectively and efficiently. Then get the straight poop. Spend the money. Prosper.

We don't claim to be research experts but we know enough to state that the following suggestions should be implemented and followed as rigorously as possible.

1. Raise the visibility of your research director within the company and listen to her. Make her the voice of your consumer and someone with considerable management clout. (If you can't do this comfortably, then you have the wrong research director.)
2. Use your outside research provider as a close partner. Listen to him. He has lots of clients and his finger is (or should be) on the pulse of the consumer. While he can't give away proprietary information from his other clients, he likely knows more about the consumer than anyone in your organization. Listen.

3. Make sure your outside research "partner" stays as objective as possible. Don't let him report what management wants to hear. Make sure his reports are accurate and demand that his opinions maintain an outside party viewpoint.

4. Regularly bring in as guest speakers other research organizations. Again, listen. Take and use all the information that is relevant to your company. You wouldn't think of driving in the dark without headlights; why would you try to sell without as much insight as possible?

5. Keep your research consistent from year to year. Don't change questions unless you have a valid reason for doing so. If you do, then try to keep the trend information as consistent as possible. We'll say it again: trends are the key to learning.

6. Be sure to include all your competitive issues in your quantitative research. You need to know where the boogeymen are hiding. You need to measure your progress against that of your competitors'—and often market share just isn't enough. Market share is a look backward in time. Marketing research gives you a bit of a chance to look into the future.

7. Be sure to include parts of the research to measure the in-house brand market segment (+20 percent of all volume in supermarkets). That way, you'll truly

begin to understand the power of your brand and whether it's growing or diminishing. We're seeing, hearing, and reading stories of the growing power of in-house brands.

Research. Love it or hate it, but do it.

12

Never Give the Gun to the Dog

CREATING GREAT ADVERTISING IS A TEAM PROCESS. TIME AND again, we'll tell you to take the effort to know (if not love) the team. Take a creative to lunch. Yes, it's true they talk with their mouths full, but do it anyway. Have a drink with a researcher. Granted, they either can't hold their liquor or will drink you under the table. Play squash with a marketer. Yes, she'll whip your butt—but she'll do it graciously. Do whatever you can to get everyone working as a team.

Steve has an analogy he likes to use that he read in Adam Smith's *Powers of Mind*. Great advertising is like hunting. You need a hunter, a dog, and a gun. Marketers are the hunters. They're the ones who decide what kind of game you're going after and which forest you'll work. Researchers are the dog. Once you tell them what you're going after, they'll do a terrific job of tracking down and cornering your target. Creatives are the gun. If the marketers and researchers do their jobs right, the creatives will hit the target every time.

Yeah, it's corny. But there's a lot of truth to it. Don't go hunting without a dog, don't give the gun to the dog, and don't try to redesign the gun while it's shooting.

13

Don't Make Focus Groups Your Creative Director

ARE YOU REALLY WILLING TO LET TEN, TWENTY, OR THIRTY consumers with no marketing or branding experience dictate your advertising plans for the next season? Think about brilliant, breakthrough advertising campaigns of the past. And not just your own. Ask yourself if you honestly think those campaigns would have survived being presented to a series of focus groups in rough form?

Focus groups have an important role to play in managing your brand. Creative director isn't one of them. And frankly, it's highly insulting to run creative work past a small group of consumers for their "top of mind" thoughts. Why not just tell the creative people, "I showed this ad to my wife last night and she hated it." (Unless your wife is the creative director of a billion-dollar advertising agency.)

Too many companies use focus groups as insecurity blankets or cover-your-ass safety checks. (Jeff thinks they are often used as muzz research so the results can be "all things to all listeners.") They use groups to "test" creative work. Big mistake. Focus groups aren't marketers or advertising professionals, they're consumers and customers.

Used properly, focus groups can take you inside the

minds and hearts of your audience in ways quantitative research never can. Focus groups can give you a sense of consumer reaction to your product or service. They can provide powerful input to your marketing, media, research, and creative people. They can tell you what emotional benefits they derive from your product or service.

They help solve an immediate issue: "What's the depth of thinking some of our best customers might have about what we're doing or propose to do?" They're also fast and relatively cheap, critical attributes in today's business practices. So they can have a good role to play in the development process, provided you make them "non-muzz" and truly usable to your own people.

And with millions of blogs springing up on the Internet, you can now even find a hot new source for consumer feedback. New research companies are springing up that can track every blog site for a mention of your product or service. It's a neat, nifty way to do real-time focus group–type surveying— and find out what people are saying about you when they think you're not listening.

Make your creative, marketing, media, and research people listen to the groups. Especially your creative people.

Make them attend. And not just the senior people. Hardly anyone watches the tapes that are provided after the groups are run. The summaries and overall conclusion often contain the biases of the moderator—and often miss the nuances that can make all the difference.

By using focus groups early in the strategic development process, you can provide everyone on your team with insights and perspectives they can't get anywhere else. The language of the consumer. Their usage process. Their likes and dislikes. Information that can be hugely valuable as you search for ways to speak to this audience.

Used properly, there's a tremendous amount of insight to be learned from focus groups. But keep in mind that focus groups are qualitative, not quantitative. And even the qualitative part is suspect as better Internet brand research tools are developed.

Good focus group moderators will point out the dangers of a group opinion leader. (That's the person in the room who rides roughshod over the quieter people's opinions. That group opinion leader should be referred to your local prosecutor as a good candidate to be a jury foreman.) In general, three or four people in a group of ten will end up putting their opinions out there, with the rest of the group nodding in agreement. (Further evidence that focus groups shouldn't be used as a substitute for quantitative research.)

Good focus group moderators will provide an objective, clear (and sometimes cautious) recap of the session. Listen to that moderator. She was in the room, not behind the glass, and believe it or not that makes a difference.

So what does it all mean? Simple. Focus groups have a place. That place is early in the process. Use them sparingly. Use them wisely. Use them early. Or don't use them at all.

A GREAT ADVERTISING STRATEGY IS THE HIDDEN GEM

"If it made sense, that would be a very powerful idea."

Napoleon had one. Alexander had one. Sun Tzu had one. Richard Nixon had one. You should have one, too. It's a strategy—a plan for getting from Point A to Point B. But just keep in mind the "fog of war." Or as they teach in the Israeli tank corps, "Make sure everyone knows the plan so it's easy to change."

If you're expecting tips on how to write a strategy statement, we invite you to take the course Steve and Jane Maas teach at the Association of National Advertisers. This isn't a section on how long a strategy statement should be, what format it should take, who should write it, or what the approval process should be. You can work out the process issues that fit your company.

What you will find is how to think through the essence of the selling rationale. When you get that right, all the other stuff (length, format, etc.) becomes less and less important.

14

"My Company's Great! My Products Are Terrific!" Besides You, Who Cares?

"WHERE DO YOU WANT TO GO TODAY?" TAHITI. HOW ABOUT you?

"Share the World with Us." No thanks, I like my world without you in it.

"Take a Seat at Our Table." Not a chance, buddy.

Do you even know whose headline or tag line those are? Do you care? Why should you?

Pick up a newspaper or magazine. Flip through it and read the headlines of the ads. All the ads, not just the ones in your industry. Keep tabs of the ones that have a benefit for the reader and the ones that just brag and claim their company or product is great and terrific.

It's the single most common mistake advertisers make. No end-user benefit, no thought about what the buyer may be interested in or want. Just pure chest pounding! "Aren't we terrific?"

Who cares?

Another variation on "our company's great our products are terrific" is the "just try it" variation. It's another form of claim that once you've tried a product you'll really want to use it. But without a reason to believe or a reason to switch, why would you try it in the first place?

This is the one advertising error that really drives Jeff up a wall. It's a completely unnecessary error that's made in haste and without rational thinking. It's the sign of an amateur advertiser. It's a colossal waste of money for the advertiser. (Oooh, Jeff's on a tear, here. But he's got a point.)

We've actually done a count and between 70 and 80 percent of all ads and commercials have this fault. Bet you come up with the same numbers we do—time and time again, year after year.

And the worst sinner of all is corporate advertising. It amazes us that the corporate brand campaign, which should be getting the attention of the most sophisticated and knowledgeable people—the CEO or COO—is generally the worst offender.

From a recent issue of *Business Week* the following are just five examples of "my company is great" headlines:

Their talent, skill and strength have been on display in 24 countries. Just like Genworth Financial.
  (*"Their" refers to Andre Agassi and his wife,
    Steffi Graff*)

We bridge the gap between performance and energy savings for customers around the world.
  (*ABB*)

Times change, but the strength of our promise remains the same.

(New York Life)

We've got the power to get the job done.

(Scottrade)

Yes, there's always a learning curve. We wear ours.

(Jefferson Wells)

The fact is, an ad that talks about how great a company is, is an easy ad to sell internally. Your boss likes it because he knows it's going to please his boss. His boss likes it because he knows it's going to please the president. The president of the company is thrilled that you've put in writing how good her company is. And everyone gets to go home at 5 PM. Nobody's got to sweat the details. Nobody's got to spend a lot of brainpower figuring out why your company, product, or service would be of any interest to the target audience. Ironically, we believe great advertising makes everyone work *except* the consumer. We believe it's important to make the value of your company transparent to the target audience. But in doing that, you might find it a tough sale within your organization.

Let's take a step back. How many times have you bought something (except Girl Scout Cookies) to satisfy the seller? (And even Girl Scout Cookies you buy because you're going to inhale a tube of mint cookies in one sitting.)

Buyers are selfish. And the consumers reading your ads are buyers, or at the least, potential buyers. They're selfish with their time, attention, and powers of memory. You need to satisfy them. You need to appeal to them and the benefits they may be interested in.

There's no way you can just create an ad that's the equivalent of a press announcement and think people will be a) interested, b) intrigued, or c) persuaded to buy or at least take an interest.

So take a look at your ads. Are the headlines all about you—or all about a benefit to the reader? We're sorry to say the odds are that you came up with the wrong answer.

15

Sell the Benefit, the Advantage, and the Feature— in That Order

EVER NOTICE HOW WHEN YOU'RE TALKING WITH SOMEONE his eyes glaze over when you start talking about yourself, but they light up when you start talking about him? (Unless you're the average male, in which case you probably have never noticed that phenomenon.) It's the same with advertising. Talk about what interests the customer—what he needs. And what he needs is a benefit!

Anyone who buys a product buys it for what it does for him or her. Not for the satisfaction of the seller. The operative question for any buyer is, "What's in it for me?"

Credit for this point has to go to the American Management Association. They run a workshop called How to Write Killer Copy, and we've never seen this concept explained as clearly as they do.

Take a sheet of paper and create three columns. Label the first one "Features," the second "Advantages," and the last "Benefits." Then start by listing a feature of your product. Under Advantages, list as many advantages as you can think of that the consumer would get from that feature. In the last column, list the consumer benefit(s) of each of those advantages.

For example, let's say you make cars. A feature might be "4-wheel anti-lock disc brakes." The advantage might be "can help the car stop faster; safer than the competitor's." The benefit? "Might save the consumer's life."

Now here's the key learning point: while advertisers generally promote the feature, talk about the advantage, and then let the consumer figure out the benefit, in real life the sale is *always* made the other way—the consumer wants to know the benefit (to them). Then (maybe) the advantage (to help justify the sale in their own mind). And, finally (if at all), the specific feature.

Why do advertisers sell in the reverse manner? Usually four reasons:

1. They're so caught up in the product and the brand image that they think what they've created is more important than what the consumer is seeking. Wrong.

2. The final approvers of the advertising have no training in marketing or sales and so assume that if they know what the feature does, then the average consumer knows as well. And the more features mentioned the more effective the advertising. Wrong.

3. The corporate lawyers have taken control of the selling process and convinced the powers that be that they can only mention features and not make promises. Wrong.

4. Everyone just wants to get the ad approved. They've learned over time that the final approver is going to want to see the product or service presented in the most favorable light, so selling the features makes everyone's job easy. Right for less hassle, but . . . wrong.

Think about your buying decisions from face-to-face discussion. What's been the tipping point in your decision to pull out the hard cold cash? Chances are it's been one of three: a need, a bargain price, a benefit that you just couldn't resist. And the bargain price would have been meaningless if the product didn't have the benefits that you were looking for.

Ask yourself whether you're selling the feature or the benefit. If it's not the benefit first, fix it! In fact, if the benefit isn't in the headline, revise it and get it there. Make the benefit the star—the one key communication point other than the brand name that gets remembered. Because not only will it be remembered, it'll be the reason to buy.

16

Separate Your Brand
from the Competition

THE BEST NEW BUSINESS PITCH JEFF EVER SAW: AN AD AGENCY
put two years of the competitors' advertising on a wall with
the brand names hidden and asked the prospective clients to
match the ad to the competitor.

Points made?

- Most of the industry's advertising was interchange-
  able.
- If the people who earned their living in the industry
  couldn't identify the brands, how in the hell could
  the consumer?

Try it yourself. Gather up all the competitive advertising,
cover up all brand recognition symbols and the logos, put
them all on the wall, and ask yourself (and your team) if they
can identify who did what.

Now here's the tough question: is your advertising any
different than anyone else's? If your advertising doesn't separate you from your competition, you're wasting your money.
(The theme "stop wasting your company's money" is another
that will recur throughout this book.)

Your brand, every brand, needs a clear, distinct point of difference. Don't get me-too'd to death.

Leo Burnett, the founder of the Chicago-based agency that bears his name, was a master of distinctive advertising. He created icons (the Marlboro Man, Charlie the Tuna, etc.) that represented his clients' brands. His spirit lives on in the GEICO gekko and Aflac's duck. Is it great advertising? Well, we remembered the clients' names, which is a start. But possibly the best thing of all is both campaigns have forced other insurance companies to sharpen their own marketing efforts. We've seen more memorable insurance company advertising in the past year than we have in the previous ten.

Seek a point of difference. What's going to make the consumer choose your brand over the competitors'? What's the point of differentiation? Maybe there isn't any—you've got a parity (or parody) product. Then your only point of differentiation is your advertising and marketing. They're 100 percent of your brand image.

Why do you choose Kellogg's Raisin Bran over Post Raisin Bran? Why do customers go to Tiffany's instead of Cartier's? Or Harry Winston over 47th Street Diamond Discount Express? Or Microsoft over Apple? eBay over Amazon? Or Amazon over eBay?

Size up your product from the consumer's point of view by asking everyone involved to provide their point of view. Fill your office with every potential competitor's product.

Bring in the sales force, the engineers, the researchers, and the marketers. Have an honest conversation. (Promise everyone that what they say in the room stays in the room. And if company politics are an issue, then ask the sales people if you can meet in *their* office. Whatever works.) Invite your vendors over. Tell them any negative comments won't result in their being dismissed.

Is your product better or worse than the competition? Can you turn its weakness into a strength? ("The only vacuum cleaner that *won't* suck up your baby by mistake.") As Baby Boomers age, their fat, clumsy fingers and failing eyesight are creating new opportunities in technology. Smart functionality can also mean "retro functionality" as manufacturers make their products simpler, easier, and with larger type and buttons for this aging, profitable demographic.

If your product's the same, then turn to the research and marketing people. What's the unique selling proposition they can come up with that will set your product apart from the competition?

Is your advertising and marketing better than your product? It can happen—and you've got to be willing to face the need to improve the product. One of the partners who worked on the Miller Brewing Company account at Backer & Spielvogel had a simple, but very ironic, photo on his wall. It was a framed blowup of a print taken at a NASCAR race. Two fans in the stands were wearing Miller hats and Miller

T-shirts. And both had a bottle of Budweiser in their hands. As that partner said to Steve, "It's my reminder, every day, of what my job is."

If your advertising, marketing, promotion, and Web site don't separate you from your competition, you're wasting your money. Just put your product in a white box and sell it on the shelf as Brand X.

Are there exceptions? Few and far between. If you're the number-one brand in the category, and you know for a fact that increasing the category size automatically gives you the lion's share of sales, then it's okay to promote the category.

If you've invented a completely new type of product that effectively creates an entire new industry, you can promote the idea of the industry. For a little while. Until you wake up one morning and find you're Kodak or IBM or Moxie or Boeing or any other company that once upon a time thought it had an iron grip on the market.

So find your difference. Turn it into a competitive advantage. And sell the difference like crazy. You would never go to a singles club to sell yourself as "just like everyone else." Why sell your brand that way?

17

Make Sure All Your Advertising Speaks with One Voice

GATHER UP ALL YOUR MARKETING AND ADVERTISING MATERI-
als and see if they're talking in the same voice and delivering
the same message. All of it. Even the dinky throwaway brochure you assigned to your junior people for that one-off promotion in Des Moines last month.

That simple brochure for the single dealer in Iowa is
a perfect opportunity to test your up-and-coming junior
people. Give the assignment to two different people. One of
them comes back with a brochure that knocks your socks off:
4-color design, new headline, new body copy. The other one
comes back with the recommendation that you take the existing brochure you did last month for another dealer, change
the local address (a simple black-plate printing change), and
ship them to Iowa. Too often, junior people think the best way
to get ahead is to be noticed and the best way to be noticed is
to do something different. For our money, we'll take the person who's thinking strategically (and economically) every
time!

Is every single piece of communication consistent? Does
it all have consistent colors and graphics (what we call "look
and feel")? Are your tag line and branding message on it? Or

did someone decide to reinvent the wheel and come up with something "creative" because this was their chance to shine? (If so, remind them, gently, that the best way to shine is to not reject the obvious.) Or worse, did your Web people go off on their own and claim, "The Web is a special case"?

Yes, there's a lot of short-term thinking out there today. Yes, we seem to all be rushing to put out fires that spring up out of nowhere. But none of that is an excuse to alter, ignore, or (worst case) abandon your brand image or your long-term marketing objectives.

All your advertising is subconsciously recognized by the consumer as building blocks in the formation of your brand's image. There's just no getting away from that fact. The world isn't a series of isolated, discreet events. And your advertising isn't even item #25 on the agenda of your customer—even if you're selling new cars and he's in the market for one. But your customer does maintain a cogent understanding of your brand and what it communicates.

With today's media fragmentation and complexity of content, building and maintaining your brand requires that you reinforce, reinforce, reinforce. No individual ad is strong enough to stand on its own. It's the totality of your marketing and advertising that truly delivers your selling message and builds your brand's image.

Yes, there are subtle differences in the way people use different media: they come to TV to be entertained; they come to the Internet for information as well as entertainment. Talking to consumers in those two different media require different levels of content, not context. Your overall brand image needs to be relevant to the context in which the consumer accesses the information. But, make sure it's all communicating the same thing.

THE CREATIVE DIRECTOR—THE CREATIVE PROCESS

"Hey, great meeting! Thanks, guys."

They've given you a raise. They've given you a corner office (on a lower floor—remember, you're only the Creative Director). They've given you new stationery and new business cards. If you're extremely lucky, they've given you an administrative assistant. But have they given you the job . . . or just the title?

Creative Director isn't just a title, it's a job description. And everyone, not just creative people, should know exactly what that job entails.

When you hire a contractor to build a house, you review other work he's done, compare his prices, and discuss the plans before he starts. But when he's on the job, you don't start telling him how to nail the timber. Give your creative director the same professional courtesy.

It's amazing how many people who speak English think that qualifies them to critique writing. Or how many people who slept through one art history class in college think that qualifies them to talk about design.

Being creative director means being in charge of the creative product. Totally in charge. If you learn how to work well with one, he or she can take your advertising to places you never imagined.

And if you are one—but now you want the job, not just the title— well, here are some tips that can put you on the road to real power.

18

Guide and Manage, Don't Design and Write

A GOOD CREATIVE DIRECTOR WILL GUIDE AND DIRECT. A GREAT creative director will guide and manage. It's a considerable difference.

Watch the ego! Anyone who's reached the level of creative director has tremendous and wide-ranging talents. The question is how she uses them to build her company, her people, and the brands for which she has responsibility.

Early in Steve's career he had a problem he didn't know how to solve, so he went to his boss. The boss's answer was short, succinct, and memorable. "If I tell you what to do, then what do I need *you* for?" he said. "Your job is to come to me, explain the problem and your suggested solutions. My job is to say 'yes' or 'no.'"

We've dealt with blowhards, pompous asses, bipolars, brilliant salesmen who couldn't manage, some who drained the life out of every concept presented to them, some who just plain couldn't do anything, and others who had once been brilliant and could do it all but had become extinct volcanoes. But when you work with a creative director who is great, it's like working with a world-class orchestra leader—the results are electrifying.

Any great creative director must have five key attributes:

1. You've gotta love advertising and the process of its development.
2. You need to be a great listener.
3. You must know how to develop talented workers and keep them loyal.
4. You've got to be honest and above internal and client politics.
5. You must love selling and be a great salesman.

The best of the best creative directors not only love advertising but have made the study of advertising a critical part of their being. They take great pride in their profession, and for them it is a profession. They clearly know the importance advertising plays in the development of brands.

For them, advertising is a critical part of business. They have no patience with those who think advertising is secondary to finance or manufacturing. (And they're enough of a businessman or woman to know a bit about those other disciplines and to be able to hold their own in a conversation with those peers.) Nor patience for those who think that advertising is something to dabble in. They know that to do great work you must work your heart out.

And that latter point is what they come to work for. Great work. Great work produced by their team, not themselves.

Second, the best creative directors are the best listeners. If you're a creative director who listens with a pencil in your hand or won't read copy without one—STOP! Your job is to listen and get the best work from your people, not to enter into a competition with them. The process is a *team* process and for the most part you're a non-playing captain.

You also need to listen to the marketers and learn everything there is to know about the market you're selling into and the strategy that will make the advertising a success. Listen to the researchers and get to know more about more aspects of the consumer than anyone else. Listen to the pop cultural world of today and know it from years gone by. And listen to your people to truly understand what they are creating, why they are creating that work, how that work will be sold, and how it will succeed in the market.

Third, it's through the listening process and the managing of your team that the best creative directors teach, mentor, and develop their team's skills and especially the skills of those who will ultimately become creative directors themselves.

A few years ago we saw a photo of David Carradine directing a movie. Taped to the side of his camera was a sign "Share the Glory." Smart advice both for himself and anyone working with him.

When was the last time someone said—out loud and in public—"You're doing a good job"? When was the last time you said that to someone else? (Outside of those horrific employee evaluation meetings.) We rarely hear employees being told they're doing a good job. How sad. We're coming to believe that praise and spot bonuses are a lost art and practice. They shouldn't be. They're critical in developing a feeling of job security and the creation of great creative. And, you'll find that giving praise and reward generates a feeling as satisfying as getting them. ("Nice job. Take your significant other for dinner on the company." Not so hard, is it?)

Can the greatest magic, the most strategic insights, the most awareness-generating and persuasive advertising get developed by the youngest (or least respected) member of the team? Absolutely. Especially if you give everyone on your team room to make mistakes and room to participate.

In Malcolm Gladwell's best-selling book *Blink,* he tells the story of women orchestra members. Although women were auditioning for major orchestras around the world, they weren't getting hired until the audition process included a screen—so the listeners couldn't know the sex or ethnicity of the auditioned. Take a page from that book: make sure you're not "creative blind" and picking work because it was done by someone "the right age," or "the right level." Great creative directors can judge the work on the basis of work alone and not get caught in the trap of promoting the work done by those who were supposed to be doing the best work.

If the solution that's presented to you doesn't solve the problem, don't try to fix the solution. Explain to the people who did the work what you think the problem is. Why you think the work doesn't solve the problem. And if they agree with you, send them back to bring you a solution that solves the problem.

To get the best and freshest work from your people, follow the advice of an art director we know: "Stay in the area of the problem, not the area of solution." The temptation is to continue to bring your style and technique to all the work that's brought to you. It's a temptation that will lead to unhappy employees, inefficiencies, and unnecessary work. As a manager you've got to learn to keep your hands off the work.

Fourth, in order to win the complete confidence of her team, management, and the client, a creative director has to be honest and above politics. She needs to say what she means and mean what she says. No bullshit. No ulterior motives. People's careers and the brand images and sales she is responsible for are too important for anything else.

Fifth—and maybe hardest of all—a great creative director needs to love selling and be a world-class salesperson. Ultimately she is the one responsible for understanding and believing that the work will successfully sell the brand and she's got to be able to sell the work through the organization and up the ladder in the client organization. She has to own it, believe in it, and sell it because if she doesn't, no one else will be able to.

Is that hard? For a nonlinear, emotional, right-brained person with an artistic background, it's the hardest part of the job. But if you want to rise in the ranks and be the best creative director you can be (and command literally millions of dollars in salary), then that's the skill set you've got to develop.

In the end, every client and marketer looks to the creative director to be able to sit down with her, one-on-one, to discuss the market, the brand, opportunities faced, the likelihood of success, and the reasons why the advertising that is about to be approved should succeed. This meeting of the minds and selling of the advertising is the pinnacle of the creative director's job. If she does it well, every member of the advertising and marketing team will share fame and fortune.

Are you ready to be a world-class creative director? Only if you are willing to breathe, eat, and sleep advertising. Are you ready to have a world-class creative director working for you? Only if you're willing to empower that person to do the job she's been hired for.

Great creative work often makes the people who have to approve it uncomfortable. It should startle and provoke. Amuse and inspire. It should make you think. Your first instinct might be to play it safe. But as a Texas politician once observed, "The only thing in the middle of the road is yellow lines and dead armadillos."

19

Get the "No-Bodies" Out of Your Approval Process

THE STEREOTYPE OF CORPORATE INEFFICIENCY HAS ALWAYS been the yes-man. But the biggest drag on resources and emotions are people we call the "no-bodies." They're the people in the chain of command who have a *no* but no *yes.* They'll tell you they have a yes. They'll kid themselves they have a yes. But the simple truth is, if they say no, the work has to be redone, altered, revised, or killed. If they say yes, all they really mean is, "It's safe for me, you can show it to my boss."

Sometimes they're someone's assistant. Or they're a director who reports to a micromanaging vice president (or a vice president who reports to a micromanaging division head). But often enough, they're simply people in the organization who've been given authority but no responsibility. As a result, they can only criticize and comment—and they feel if they don't make criticisms or comments (even if the work is on target, on strategy) then they're not doing their job.

Usually, the effect of the no-bodies is felt by outside suppliers. It's especially true in the dealings between advertising agency and client. If you work with an advertising agency (or run one yourself), make sure you haven't created the "*N*-structure." The *N*-structure was first pointed out to Jeff by

Ken Roman, at the time the CEO of Ogilvy & Mather. Ken's written a whole bunch of helpful, smart books on advertising, so it's no surprise he noticed this pattern in dealing with certain clients.

The *N*-structure happens when work starts at the lowest rung of the agency (the bottom left of the *N*), moves its way up the left side of the *N* rung by rung to the president of the agency, then amazingly and frustratingly slides down the middle of the *N* to the very bottom on the client side (the bottom right of the *N*) where it needs to work its way up the client's chain of command. This is almost an insane process. The work goes from the proven expert on advertising, the agency president, to in many cases an assistant product manager fresh out of college who has only months of experience.

It's wearing. It's idea and spirit killing. It costs untold millions in time and money wasted. At almost every step of the way, each person feels an obligation to make some comment or emendation, which just delays the deliverables and demoralizes the suppliers.

What's a simple test? Take a look at your production schedule for recent projects: if the approval schedule is longer than the creative schedule, then you've got a whole group of no-bodies in your system.

Take a look below and above you. Ask yourself how many people you have in the process who are putting in their opinions without having any responsibility to really approve the work? Get 'em out of the loop! Either make them responsible for giving the go-ahead or don't let them pass judgment on the work being presented.

Or do what we heard a freelance designer did. He had a flat fee of $1,000 for everything he did. Whether it was a one-fold brochure for a dealer or a corporate annual report. In the fine print on his deal was this: his fee was $1,000 for every person who had to approve the work. So simple brochures usually cost $2,000 and annual reports would run $20,000 or more!

Tough to get the no-bodies out of the loop? You bet. Especially when you realize how many times in your workday you yourself are a no-body. So start with yourself. The hardest thing a manager has to learn is not to wade into the work. At all times, you should be able to step back and ask yourself, "Am I making this better, or just different?" A bad manager somehow always believes he's making it better. A good manager will sometimes admit he's making changes because they're what he would do if he were doing it himself or because he thinks his boss would approve. A great manager will think about whether the changes he's about to suggest will make any significant difference—and will pick his battles accordingly.

Once you've reined yourself in, take a look at your direct reports. If you don't trust them enough to let them approve work without your seeing it, then why are they in the process? Tell them to bring you the work and then listen in while the work is presented.

You can then mentor them and monitor them. If they're overmanaging (or undermanaging), give your approval (or disapproval) to the work—and then, privately, give your employees some coaching on how they should have handled the problem. But don't let them learn at the expense of either the people presenting work or your company's efficiency. (By the way, cutting out the no-bodies will save your company a pile of money.)

When you've removed the no-bodies from your area of command, start working your way up the line. Ask yourself where you're expected to be a no-body: where do you have responsibility, but no authority? Then start managing up (and managing your career). Find ways to make it clear to your boss(es) that you should either have the authority to go with the responsibility or you shouldn't have the responsibility.

A word of caution: Be smart—do that as diplomatically (or politically) as you can. You don't want as many jobs on your resume as Steve has. Seriously, given the everyday crunch of time, constant process reengineering, and the unrelenting search for cost savings, eliminating no-bodies is a clear win for all involved.

20
Walk the Halls

WE PRACTICED IT FOR YEARS. EVERY MANAGEMENT BOOK WE read says do it. We repeat the message here for those who don't do it and haven't read about it. Walk the halls; talk to those in the trenches—in their offices or other informal, comfortable circumstances.

The best advertising (and everyone's best work for that matter) is created in a secure and supportive environment. Communication from the top to the bottom and (very important) from the bottom to the top helps create that environment. So put "walk the halls" on your calendar, do it at least twice a week for at least two hours and spend some time with at least five people that you don't normally meet with during that time.

It's important to walk the halls when things are good and when they're not so good. It's absolutely essential to walk the halls when they're terrible. And don't seek out the same people over and over again. Make sure you meet with everyone over the course of time.

What are the benefits? There are lots of them.

1. Staffers will get to know you and feel comfortable. That generates better work.

2. You'll have a chance to stress the goals and direction of the company in a truly persuasive environment. That helps spread the word and makes the goals more achievable.

3. You'll be able to snuff out politics and rumors at the level they start. Never underestimate the importance of snuffing out or confirming rumors.

4. You'll learn who the key players are in your company. Staffers always praise those that are best.

5. You'll learn more about the client and his demands than you can ever know from your top lieutenants. Just take what you hear from them with a grain of salt.

6. You'll learn how accurate the information is that you are getting from your top lieutenants. But don't undercut them—use the information to help make them even better performers.

7. You'll learn more about the quality of work that is being created than you ever could by just having it presented to you in your office in a far more formal presentation.

Steve had a boss who taught him the true art of hall walking: "Walk the halls at 7 PM; it'll take you to the problem every time." His theory was that the people who were still there at that time were either a) the dedicated employees staying late to clean up someone else's mess or b) the problem employees who were overwhelmed and couldn't manage their jobs. Either way, the conversations he would have with the 7 PM people would often reveal the organizational issues. (Sadly, we've also learned that those conversations also reveal the people whose home life is a disaster.)

Does it have to be hall walking? Not always. Jeff's a great believer in buying the creatives a drink. Moving the conversation outside the office and behind a martini often lets people relax and talk about the real issues. Often, when Steve is frustrated with a client, Jeff will take him out for an Irish whiskey.

So . . . be comfortable, be smart, be seen—and listen, listen, listen.

21
Share Information

AS WE SAID IN POV #2, THINKING OUTSIDE THE BOX IS PRO-bably a waste of time. But thinking outside your cubicle can pay huge dividends.

Always look for ways to extend the use, life, and value of any marketing materials created by anyone in the company. With the hundreds of ways to reach consumers these days, there's no shortage of ways you can apply similar marketing materials and ideas to disparate applications.

We're big proponents of weekly staff meetings. Steve likes to run them without chairs to make sure they're short. Jeff likes to run them with a predistributed agenda to make sure they're focused. Either way, the objective's the same.

Each person in the room says what they're working on, who they're working with (outside vendors, in-house departments), and what the purpose of the project is. Everyone listens with two objectives in mind:

1. "Can I use this material?" Each person should be asking whether the work can be applied somewhere else. Would a brochure being done for dealers make a smart addition to the Web site? Would a sell-sheet for

consumers work for third-party sales by simply changing the copy? (Thereby saving printing and design costs.) Everyone should be listening with an ear toward multiple applications of marketing materials.

2. "Can someone else use this material?" Besides thinking of how you might use the idea, you should also be listening for ways other people can use the same idea. People tend to become territorial and develop "not invented here" thinking. Having everyone thinking about how different ideas can cross-pollinate helps break down the "mine! mine!" mentality and inspires more team effort.

It's an effective way to put the power of the department to work or to keep everyone on track in your agency or group. With everyone sharing what they're working on, it's easy for people to see potential synergies, and it's a smart way to keep you abreast of what everyone's doing.

Often, different departments are given parallel assignments. Without a system in place to cross-reference the work, a company ends up paying twice for something that could have been easily modified for both users. Ironically, it's the outside vendors who often know the score: they're working on different projects for the same company and are reluctant to make the combining suggestion, as it will cut into their profits. Senior management should review its list of all outside vendors and consider consolidation, either of the vendors or of the assignment list. That will give you some measure of control over both costs and type of work being done.

And being in control is one of the first steps in being a good manager.

22

Partner with the Research Department—They'll Lead You to the Consumer Every Time

TAKE A RESEARCHER TO LUNCH.

Yes, they talk funny. Yes, they dress funny. Yes, you might be teased by your cohorts. But here's the bottom line: Consistent, realistic, actionable consumer research is worth its weight in gold for the development of strong brands and great advertising. The key word in the previous sentence is "actionable."

No ifs, ands, or buts about this. If you don't have a strong consumer research department supporting you and the brand, you're always going to struggle. If you succeed without it, it'll only be because of luck and against the odds. Charley Ryant, a great creative director at Backer & Spielvogel, used to have a sign on his wall that said "Guts is cheaper than research." At the time, Steve laughed and thought it was right on the money. Ten years and five agencies later, he learned it was the most foolish aphorism he'd ever seen in the business.

In an era of staff reductions, budget cuts, and the ever-growing use of focus groups as a substitute for in-depth knowledge, you must—repeat, must—use research to stay ahead of the curve. The consumer is ever more sophisticated, society is more complicated and moves at lightning speed, and reaching your target audience is a lot harder than you think. Outstanding research is essential. It's critical that creatives learn to understand and appreciate its value.

Outstanding research leads straight to the heart and soul of the consumer's values, lifestyle, and buying decision process. It brings you in touch with her, and makes her as familiar to you (in terms of your knowledge and understanding of her motivations and actions) as your favorite cousin. And that makes selling to her a quantifiable and repeatable skill. It turns advertising from a supposed black box into a business process that can be depended on and managed professionally and consistently.

Repeatable, iterative processes are the key to any successful business. Henry Ford figured that out over a hundred years ago. If you don't have a system in place that makes you an expert on your target audience so you can intelligently plan to achieve your marketing objectives, then you're always going to be playing catch-up. Ad hoc may work for a while in boom times, but it's a sure road to disaster when the economy turns lean and mean.

But for research to be outstanding, it's got to be usable. And not just to the research people, but the entire company. And no one can use it more than the creative department.

No one can create in a vacuum. The more information you have, the more creative you can be. It's a truism that frustrated managers and floundering creative folk often just don't understand. But when your creatives fill blank screen time with nothing intrinsically important, when you depend on borrowed interest that's unlikely to successfully sell, when you start reaching for celebrity endorsers or old music rights, that's when you'll begin to catch on that without good research your work's only as good as your boss's mood on the day you present to him. And let's not even mention "self-esteem."

There's no such thing as too much information. It leads to more ideas, more relevant ideas, more selling concepts, and a more persuasive selling message.

There's a wealth of information contained in most research reports. There's also a huge body of useful knowledge inside the head of every research person. In both cases, you have to dig it out and translate it in order to use it.

That's why we tell creatives to "take a researcher to lunch." Learn to ask them questions about what the research says and what it's trying to tell you about the consumer. Have the research department become your partner in understanding the consumer. If possible, ask them to write those thoughts in plain English, in a style that will personalize the consumer. Somewhere in that conversation (*not* a presentation) a lightbulb will go off in the creative person's head. Somewhere in that conversation the meaning of the data (from a creative point of view) will be understood. And in that synthesis that creative people do so well and marketing and research people can never understand, the creatives will begin to see how to translate the data into usable information to create award-winning advertising that works. It's a eureka moment that comes from the gathering of lots of information, hard thinking, and hours of putting thoughts on paper/computer screen.

That's the moment when you'll recognize that research isn't a threat. In fact, researchers are the best job partners you can have. They're your support in terms of making you smart: they actually have the tools to validate how you use that knowledge to successfully communicate and sell. They make you more valuable. (Yes, that same validation research could show your creative work is not effective, but you can't live your life in fear. Be good, be strong, and if necessary learn from your mistakes.)

Yes, researchers speak a language of methodology. They load their reports up with verbatims, questionnaires, and statistics. Then they write an executive summary aimed at the marketing people, often pretty useless to the creative people. Which makes the creative people think there's nothing in the report of any value to them. WRONG!

It's not easy to become friends with them. They dress funny. They talk in jargon. They're no fun. They're often rigid and opinionated. Well, hello? Sound like you from the other side? Duh.

We're not asking you to marry these people. We're saying great creative work is developed with the help of a team and the research people are critical members of that team. They should become your closest on-the-job friends. You need to work with them so they never again bring you the bad news that a focus group in Omaha just killed your award-winning campaign.

Now a few words for the marketing managers' perspective.

Time and time again we hear the complaint that their advertising says nothing, isn't even close to being persuasive, but costs a fortune. Frustration reigns, and the idea of cost cutting always comes to the fore.

Further, the marketing manager sees every one of his peers in other corporate domains tracking measurements in every aspect of their businesses. Business processes have truly gone through a revolution and it's inevitable that marketing and advertising will need to catch up. It's time for the marketing manager to admit that *if you can't measure it you can't manage it.* It's time for him to speak up and become the professional he needs to become. And he needs to convince his team that, indeed, measurement will become essential in everything they do.

Be prepared to get judged on facts and figures. Is it hard? Is it expensive? You bet.

Your researchers, creatives, and marketers need to learn how to work together.

YOU NEED ALL THREE TYPES TO CREATE EFFECTIVE, BREAKTHROUGH ADVERTISING!

We wrote that in capital letters. We're also going to say it again because it's one of the key pieces of information in this book: You need all three types working as a team to create effective, breakthrough advertising. Great advertising is always a team effort. Jeff (that's right, the account guy, not the creative) believes great work can never be created by a committee. (Now you know why Steve loves working with Jeff.) But brilliant creative work comes when it's supported by a team. Art director. Copywriter. Account executive. Research director. Media planner. The important thing is to never confuse "team" with "committee."

Creatives: Find a researcher who can be your trusted friend and advisor, who can turn the data into information in a language that you as a creator understand and can build off of.

Researchers: Speak up, get involved, take the initiative. It's time to leave your cubicles. You are a vital team player.

Marketers: Wake up. Focus groups alone aren't going to do it from now on. It's time to go back to the basics and the facts. Research is a critical member of the brand team and essential to the creation of great advertising. Just remember Tip #12: never give the gun to the dog.

Team effort. And if the idea of taking a researcher to lunch still makes you shudder, pick an off-the-beaten-path restaurant.

23

Make Friends with a Media Planner

AFTER YOU'VE GOTTEN TO KNOW A RESEARCHER, ADD A MEDIA director to your list of lunch buddies.

Think of media directors as an evolutionary step between research director and human being.

Because the media director often has to meet with the client, they're usually better than the researcher at translating the research data into information a creative person can use.

Be warned: Like researchers, they love their numbers. They'll want to quickly digress (or degenerate) into "HUTS" and "homes passed" and "eyeballs." (To use some TV ratings jargon. And, there's a slew of that jargon for each and every medium.) But again, if you can keep them on track and focused on your issues, they're a font of information about where your audience is. And like the research director, if you can keep them on target, eventually they will say something that will set a lightbulb off in your head and lead you to consumer insights you can't get anyplace else.

So take a media director to lunch. Besides, they've usually got as big an expense account budget as you do, so there's a good chance they'll pick up the check.

———

One caveat: Watch out for the media guy who goes overboard on the hot new medium, program, or publication. Even with today's astoundingly rapid consumer acceptance and use of new media and new tools for accessing those media, old media should still likely be the foundation of your advertising media plans.

24

Become an Expert on the Consumer

THE VERY FIRST TIP IN THIS BOOK WAS "KNOW WHO YOUR Customers Are." Vitally important for research and marketing people. But the creative director has an even harder job: you've got to know your customer in ways no other person in the company understands.

We've hinted at this thought earlier, but here it is in black and white: The only way to understand the consumer and how she lives, what she desires, what she buys, and how she consumes media and understands the message is to participate in her life.

Get out of Manhattan (or any other big city that you live in). Lose your East-of-the-Hudson, big-city myopia. Get into the heart of this country. Fly to a midsize city, get in the car, and drive. Eat lunch in the local diner, talk to people, read the local newspaper, go to stores and talk to people in the aisles. Get to know America. Understand it so you become an expert and can communicate your view in a precise and quotable manner.

Steve once worked with an account executive who always arrived for focus groups a day early. He'd drive around until he found a cop and then ask where the best breakfast hash joint was. The next morning, bright and early, he'd plant himself at the counter and would conduct his own informal "focus groups" for an hour or two, getting to know his audience in ways no research could ever tell him.

A trip like the one above should be scheduled twice a year for your first year in creative management and then at least once a year after that. And if your research department can pull together one or two informal groups to discuss what the respondents are thinking about in their lives—no advertising, just life in general—that would be a major plus.

When the hands-on information from these trips is combined with the hard data from all the research we've mentioned earlier in the book, you'll begin to have a definitive, experiential understanding of your target consumer. If you don't, you're either misunderstanding the world you're now participating in or your research is faulty. Find out what the right answer is (it will take some good thinking), and fix the problem!

You'll then be able to serve as a translator between research, the client, the account people, and your creative team to make sure that everyone understands the consumer and everyone is on the same page in knowing how to talk to her.

And once you determine who the stars, or potential stars, of your creative department are, present them with their own opportunity for a mid-America trip. It's a great reward that will also serve the company and the client for a long time. Red states elect presidents. They also buy products.

25

Monthly Luncheon Learning Sessions

PIZZA IS THE MOST POWERFUL MANAGEMENT TOOL EVER INvented; use it generously and wisely.

Candid, off-the-record discussions (over pizza) about advertising in general, your category specifically, and your brand efforts in particular are essential to producing great advertising.

Why? Because they're fun, they generate ideas, they maintain team focus, they build camaraderie, and they eventually point out if the emperor has no clothes.

So how do you find out if you're nude? How do you start these monthly meetings given that everyone is stressed out, under great time pressures, just about sick of seeing each other, and the politics—oh the politics.

The Japanese have the perfect custom. When coworkers go out for the evening, if the bottle's on the table, anything that happens that night is tactfully forgotten the next day. In the U.S., a box of pizza should do the same thing.

The combination of pizza and soda (beer if your company allows), immediately says "friendly, casual, and off the record." It announces that the meeting is SAFE! And the team leader needs to put her reputation on the line regarding this point. This is a time for teamwork and constructive discussion. Tough stays civil; hard words stay polite; everything stays in the room.

No delaying the meeting, no missing the meeting, no arriving late. Full participation and preparation is guaranteed by each member being required to either report or comment on something.

Finally, make the meeting an open discussion. Give the meeting and the participants a chance to feel comfortable. Talk casually. Talk about good movies, bad movies. Good books. New music. Talk about great advertising and marketing campaigns past or present. And as the team gets comfortable with these sessions you can talk about your own marketing and advertising. What's working? What's not working? And why people think that.

After running successful meetings within the department over a reasonable course of time (six to nine months) it's then OK to invite peers from other departments into the meeting to give them a chance to discuss what is working and what needs to be improved from their perspective.

What we've seen is that the most important points that come to the fore at beer and pizza meetings are:

- *Process controls:* Nearly everyone has process problems over the course of a year. These meetings are a great time to get the issues on the table and to find a way to resolve them so they don't get in the way of creating great work.

- *Client relations:* Whether your client is an internal one or outside the organization, there's always bitching and moaning about the client. It's essential to recognize (and yes, trite but true) that without the client you have no job. But this is an opportunity to discuss what the client's motivations are, to share with others how you might be able to better handle his personality and address his concerns and motivations—to enable you to do your best work.

- *Category advertising that's better than yours:* This is always a showstopper in terms of "their company is easier to work for than ours." Bullshit! They're no better, or shouldn't be. These meetings are designed to get your organization changed for the better. You should be the company who is seen as having the greener grass.

Keep the meeting casual. Keep it friendly. Keep it constructive. Get to like and trust each other. Build pride in the organization. Build pride in the quality of the work. Establish benchmarks to make the work better. It's how business should be conducted. No one can create great advertising alone. No one can create it in an environment that isn't comfortable, safe, and encouraging.

So find a good local pizza parlor—and start managing by the slice.

26

Watch Videos and Go to the Movies Together

EVEN IF YOU CAN'T SCHEDULE A REGULAR MONTHLY PIZZA session, at least take the time to catch a "nooner" together now and then. The PG-13 kind, not the X-rated kind.

First, the team benefits from the camaraderie of shared experience. Second, you let the team feel as if you're all in this together and it's not just a daily grind. Third, you stay on top of what's new and hot.

Advertising and marketing don't shape popular culture; good advertising mirrors it. And the best advertising senses the early shifting winds or catches the tide before it crests.

What's new in music? Watch Fuse. What's hot in fashion? Go to a runway show. What's the new trend in editing and special effects? Go to the movies. Sharing pop culture with your crew will keep them—and you—on top of what's hot. Take the time to talk about it over beer afterward. What did different people like and hate about the film? What new trends did anyone note? Don't make it a homework assignment—keep the conversation casual and light. But stay focused on what you're trying to get from the experience: knowledge you can apply in your own marketing world.

Another point to make here is that our country seems to

be fragmenting into smaller and smaller segments with less and less entertainment in common. We seem to be losing our national icons or common thought. Part of that is the tenor and harsh voice of politics, part of that is our growing time stresses, and part is our individual entertainment media (think Ipod).

So any time spent trying to pull together your team's knowledge about our entertainment vehicles to make your advertising more pertinent to more people is a decided plus.

So log on to the local listings and pick a hot film opening this Friday!

27

Underpromise and Overdeliver

THE HEAD OF SALES COMES TO THE HEAD OF MARKETING AND asks for a brochure for the new tractor. The tractor's been in the planning and design stage for three years, but no one thought marketing needed to be called in or an ad agency notified until a month before the upcoming trade show. (That's the subject of a whole 'nother book.) Marketing and sales then meet with the creative people. They want to know how fast the brochure can be done.

You know it should take two weeks to write and design, a week for approval, and two weeks for production. But because you had an inkling that this might happen, you've already been talking to suppliers and know you can cut the schedule to three weeks. You tell them "three weeks" and they leave, satisfied, knowing they'll have the brochure with a week to spare.

Big mistake.

You should have looked at the schedule, explained that it should normally take five weeks (an honest comment), and then promised them you'd have it for them two days before the show.

Yes, they'll be uncomfortable with the deadline. Yes, they'll ask if you can do better. Yes, you'll say you'll do your best. But you should always give yourself room for the unexpected.

If you promise them three weeks and it takes three and a half, you'll look unreliable. Even though they'll have the brochure in time for the convention, those two or three extra days are going to drive them and you nuts. They'll be calling you every hour. They'll be fretting. They'll be wondering if you're the right person for the job. And when the brochures are finally delivered, they'll be annoyed that they had to worry.

If you know it can be done in three weeks by pulling out all the stops and being lucky and you tell them "three and a half," two magical things can happen:

1. The job goes remarkably smooth and it's ready in three weeks. You deliver the job and the marketing and sales people are *thrilled* that you got it to them even faster than they expected. (Of course they'll then think you can do every similar job in their unreasonable timetable! That's life.)
2. The job runs into some snags (that's Murphy's Law) and it takes the full three and a half weeks. You deliver the job exactly when you said you would. The marketers and sales people are happy that they can rely on you to deliver what you said when you said.

Win-win. No fret. No fuss. You either look like a hero or you look reliable. Not a bad choice at all, especially on your annual review.

28

Know What Your Suppliers Are Talking About

HOW LONG DOES IT TAKE TO PROGRAM MACROMEDIA FLASH? Can all your customers run it on their computers? What's the difference between lithography and offset printing? Which costs more? Which takes longer? Can you picture in your mind the difference between a camera tracking shot and a pan?

It's easy to say, "Those are just the details" and let the production people worry about it. But as the architect Mies van der Rohe used to say, "God is in the details." Or as the common expression goes, "the Devil is in the details."

If you're in advertising and marketing, you've got to know the language and the methods of every form of production. Web design and animation. Video. Film. Editing. Printing, photography—all of it. You should also understand the technology behind every form of communication from radio and TV, to Internet, WiFi, Blackberry, PDAs, and beyond.

First, if you don't know the language you're going to look, feel, and sound like an idiot. (Reason enough.) More important, understanding the production process will make you smarter about timing and cost. Every choice that's offered, every alternative that's presented, affects price and time. Unless you know what they're talking about, you're going to either end up making a promise you can't keep or becoming frustrated when things take longer and cost more than you imagined.

Once upon a time in this business it was different. Work was presented to people as hand-drawn layouts. Everyone had to use their imagination to understand what the final product would look like. It was up to the art director to bring her vision to life, quite often to the surprise of the client. ("I didn't think it would look like *that*.")

The computer, desktop publishing, desktop editing, and video editing changed the game. And they've all had unintended consequences.

If an art director shows you a computer-generated layout, it looks "finished." Unless you understand how Adobe Illustrator, Photoshop, and Quark work, you have no idea what the process is to turn that seemingly "finished" design into an actual ad. If you did, you would hesitate before making what you think are simple requests such as, "Could we see it in blue?" You'd also understand why it's going to take another two days to produce the actual finished piece.

Ditto for desktop editing. Unless you understand the entire videotape production process, you're going to be frustrated by the time and money it's going to take to turn that seemingly finished video into a truly finished film.

Know the language. Know the territory. It'll also keep you from being sold a bill of goods.

29
Learn New Tricks

THEY SAY YOU CAN'T TEACH AN OLD DOG NEW TRICKS. WELL, you better learn new tricks or you'll just be an old dog.

The brilliant TV advertisers who don't understand how people use the Internet and other new media are rapidly going the way of the print and radio gurus of the 1940s who thought TV was just radio in pictures.

Every twenty years or so the old rules need to get rewritten—and boldly. What you need to know is which old rule to keep, which rules to rewrite, and why you need to rewrite them in order to rewrite them well.

The world of advertising is in the middle of a significant change. The Internet, media on demand, and other forms of advertising (or abilities to avoid advertising) have been created. And the ever-increasing capability of all of us to multi-task has made gaining and keeping attention ever harder if not well-nigh impossible.

You hear talk about convergence? Well, you don't have to look any further than how a typical high schooler does her homework: she comes home, boots up the computer, puts her headset on, and starts playing her music. Then she logs on to AIM (AOL Instant Messenger) and starts chatting with her buddies while she tunes the TV to MTV without the sound to watch and talk about the video . . . all of that while writing her term paper on Microsoft Word and eating a low-carb snack.

And how different is it trying to reach an adult in his car, in heavy traffic, with satellite radio on, a cell phone ringing, and a cup of hot steaming coffee in hand?

It's clearly time to reinvent some rules. The question is, where do you start?

1. Hunt the marketing and advertising bookshelves and read, read, read. Read the old classics by David Ogilvy, Fairfax Cone, and others. Read the current books and listen to what the current gurus have to say and how that compares to some of the past greats.

Some great new marketing books have valid points to make; others are bogus or pure drivel. Not all will apply to your current position or situation, but even the worst of them usually has something of value that you can apply in your day-to-day work.

2. Teach a course to young people. There's nothing like kids who don't know the rules to teach you to stop having so many of your own. Teach as many kids as you can.

3. Attend occasional seminars in areas you know nothing about. Sit in on the annual meeting of the Society of Neurosurgeons, or the annual trade show of the National Association of Home Builders. Attend the breakout sessions, drifting from one to another. You probably won't understand a lot of what's being said—and that's just the point. When you start to realize how much you don't know, it will keep your mind open to new possibilities. (This is yet another call to get out of your office and delve into the world. Your life isn't what the world revolves around.)

4. Make a friend of a market researcher. Discuss your thoughts and your learning. Learn from what she's seen out in the real world.

5. Listen to your bosses and your peers. Wherever you work there is good learning and bad learning to think through. Determine what to keep and apply in the future and what to throw away. Think and don't be afraid of change.

Steve, in one of his young, brash, and arrogant days (and there were many), once thought he knew everything there was about how to make ads. He'd hired an art director fresh out of college and they were working together as a team. Steve was coming up with headlines and they were struggling to think of the visuals. Then one day, the art director burst into tears. "I don't know how to work this way," she cried. "I've always started with the pictures." They tried working through the visuals first—and they did great work together. He's a far better writer because of that day. Or at least he thinks he is.

6. Read an array of novels. Good novels, bad novels, and especially a range of novels from the day's most popular and successful novelists. They clearly have their fingers on the pulse of society. Understand what makes them so successful and what lines their pockets with hard cold cash, because in the end, that's what you're trying to do for your clients, your company, and yourself.

7. Surf the Internet. Study the layouts, navigate through site after site. Think about the ads, the pop-ups, and the pop-unders. What works and doesn't work.

8. Prowl the blogs and eZines. There's some really terrible stuff out there, but there's also some brilliant work. In fact, why not start your own—and break every rule you obey in your working life.

The more you know the more you're worth. Not every problem can be solved with the old rules. Often the old rules just get you mired in the day-to-day muck. Be bold, be daring—but know your stuff before you take that leap and know exactly why you've taken it and where it might lead. (And be sure the new rule is truly a rule and will lead to an iterative process.)

If you're lucky enough to have taken the leap at the right time, you'll find yourself at the pinnacle of advertising success.

Happy learning.

TV COMMERCIALS

"*Bill did the voice-over for this commercial.*"

Television used to be the fastest, most effective way to introduce a new product. It isn't today. It might be again tomorrow. Or it might go the way of radio and remain a profitable, important, but marginal medium. Regardless, it's still important. Even more important is getting the message right.

You've got fifteen or thirty seconds. You're in a crowded, competitive environment. You're talking to consumers who can ignore you in a hundred different ways—from fast-forwarding to switching channels to going to the bathroom.

Whatever method they choose, there are still ways to get in under their radar screens. And we've got six that might help give your TV spots a little more impact.

(Most of these tips will also be relevant to commercials targeted to users on devices such as cell phones.)

30

Shit, My Hair's on Fire!

WORKING ON PROCTER & GAMBLE IN THE 1970S AND 80S, ONE of their most important concerns was how to grab the viewer's attention. What's the setup in the first three seconds? We used to refer to it as "shit, my hair's on fire." That opening line, sound, silence, image, situation—whatever device you use—has got to grab their attention. Or as Lyndon Johnson once said, "Grab them by their balls and their hearts and minds will follow." He'd have made a damned good adman.

Or as David Ogilvy once said (with a bit more panache), "You can't save souls in an empty church."

One of our seminars is called On A.I.R. Wisdom™. "A.I.R." stands for Attention, Interest, and Recall. If you think about it, that's what any good commercial should do: get the viewers' attention, hold their interest, and help them recall your sales message and brand. In that order. You've got to get their attention before you can hope to sell them.

DVRs. Remotes. Short attention spans. Picture-in-picture. Multitasking. It's hard to generate attention. But it's critical—and it's critical to do it in good taste.

The American consumer is getting more and more jaded, more resistant, and more immune to TV advertising. We figure you've got even less than the old three-second rule to grab and hold the viewer's attention. (And, it appears that P&G is agreeing. Jeff, while editing this chapter, heard that P&G is cutting back a bit on its TV advertising to go more directly to the consumer via media such as the supermarket itself.)

As you create (approve) your commercial, ask yourself whether the opening can grab and hold the audience's attention.

How? As many different ways as there are imaginative creative people:

- Start with an unusual visual. Get the viewer to wonder what is happening. (But not a visual that has absolutely nothing to do with the benefit or solution. The former is called "vampire video"; the latter is called "borrowed interest." Yes, we know the jargon's not easy!)
- Use a sound effect that rivets attention.
- Use music that rivets attention.
- Start with compelling words.
- Use a form of blank airtime to again get the viewer to wonder what is happening.
- Create a memorable moment.
- Use unusual casting.
- Use an unusual voice-over.

In one form or another, every great advertiser, marketer, and promotion person knows how to find and use that grabber. Whether it's the promise of "free" or "0% financing" or "Psst, wanna buy a bridge?," it's the opening gambit designed to hold the viewer's attention. And today you need it more than ever.

Today's younger audiences have shorter attention spans. It's something we call "GenY velocity"—the tolerance younger audiences have for faster pacing, more cuts in a commercial, even fifteen-second and ten-second spots. The Internet, MTV, video games, and extreme sports have all trained younger viewers to expect that rhythm—and its speed of action is only growing.

Look for it. Learn it. Delve into the media your target audience uses. And get the feel for the way they literally consume information. The Internet, video games, MTV, extreme sports, video phones, etc., have all trained young people to have a higher threshold of needed excitement to gain attention. Become a student of those media and begin to understand what works and what doesn't.

Become a part of the technology culture and you'll become a more valuable player in the communication culture. (Also keep your eye out for the other side of the spectrum: the "slacker" mentality of "nothing" that was captured so well by the TV series *Seinfeld*.)

And finally, keep the attention getting in good taste. Bad taste can create tremendous attention. The kind neither you nor your company nor, most important, your brand needs. You want to get attention—you don't want to get the attention of the ten o'clock news and the FCC.

31

Don't Forget the Benefit

IF THERE'S ONLY ONE THING YOU TAKE AWAY AFTER READING this book, let it be that you include, stress, highlight, successfully communicate the single most important consumer benefit of the product or service that you are selling—in every ad that you write, approve, or pay for. Consumer benefit. Consumer benefit. Consumer benefit.

Yes, we know. We started the book saying brand, brand, brand. And now we're talking benefit, benefit, benefit. Are we changing the rules? Not really. If you think about it, they're really two parts of the same idea: it's the benefit to the consumer that shapes their perception of the brand. Give them satisfaction and they'll rate your brand highly every time.

There's just no way you can consistently and successfully sell without telling the customer what valued benefit she'll be receiving if she buys your service or product. After all, what is she buying? Not stuff! Not something just to have. She's buying something that's important to her. She's giving up cold, hard-earned cash to buy something that she thinks will make her life better and easier in some way. Your job is to find out what that need is and then sell it to her. Hard.

And interestingly, you'll find that the more important the

benefit is to the customer, the more she will want to know about that benefit and how it can help her. The more interested she is, the more she will seek out information and the more responsive she will be to your persuasion.

It sounds like we're just talking about packaged goods advertising here. Not really. Every buyer is seeking a benefit, whether it's a consumer or a corporation. If you're doing business-to-business advertising, you've still got to make the sale to *someone*. Whoever that person is, the CEO, the CFO, the head of IT—that person needs a reason to believe. They need a benefit to justify the money they're going to spend on your product or service. You've got to give them a reason to buy your brand versus your competitor's.

So how do you sell that benefit? (It usually isn't enough just to bluntly state it.) Empathy, empathy, empathy . . . resolution.

For a product to have a benefit, the consumer must have a need. Remind her of that need, demonstrate the solution, and make the sale. It doesn't have to be literal. An emotional takeaway by the consumer could just be, "Hmmm, these guys could solve my problem."

How many benefits can a product or brand have? Interesting question. The product or service itself will have many benefits. Add the brand name to the product or service and even more benefits will be discovered because the brand brings its own benefits to the selling process.

Your job is to find the benefit(s) with the most leverage. First, among all products or services in the category in which you are selling. And second, among the considered set of choices that the customer will bring as alternates to your particular brand.

One thing to learn about commercials, thirty-second ones, is that when produced brilliantly they absolutely allow you time to give viewers an experience of the product. We're not talking "demonstration" here (that's so 1950s, kids), we're talking "experience." Maybe of the product. Maybe of its benefits.

We had a friend who was the Queen of Fragrances—a longtime creative director who developed not just the advertising, but even the product names and concepts. As she used to say to us, "Every fragrance commercial is just one long product benefit. The hard part is figuring out yet another new way of saying 'Wear our fragrance and the man of your dreams will show up.'"

Joe Sedelmeier, the Chicago-based commercial director who helped create some great commercials (Wendy's "Where's the beef?" to name just one) used to mock the traditional commercial structure:

April has a problem. May, who's standing right next to her in the kitchen, just happens to have the client's product in her purse. May whips out the product. The commercial cuts away to July's voice-over demonstration of the product. Cut back to a smiling April shaking

hands with May and thanking May for saving her life.
So 1950s!

Joe's brilliance was his ability to assess a storyboard and then cut to the heart of the product's benefit. He was a master at it, generally rewriting the storyboards that were submitted to him. "Where's the beef?" is a classic example: he found the competitor's weakness (and the consumer's complaint) versus his client's product and then he pounded home the point. His "headline" became a phrase used in everyday language for years.

By the way, if you or the client can't come up with a benefit, either you haven't done your homework or the brand shouldn't be advertised. And we'll bet the error is in the lack of homework and research. We see it time and time again.

This isn't new news. More than seventy years ago, Rosser Reeves invented something he called the Unique Selling Proposition (U.S.P.) and then built his ad agency into a billion-dollar brand—selling the Unique Selling Proposition as his agency's Unique Selling Proposition.

He found a unique way of describing it, but he was talking about the thing every good marketing and advertising person learns: you've got to find a unique benefit for your product or service and then use it to sell your customer.

Identifying benefits through seat-of-the-pants methodology leads to advertising that talks about yourself. When you're ready to get serious about finding the brand benefit that will become your powerful selling tool you need to turn to research.

Here's an example of where focus groups would be helpful: discussing possible alternate benefit promises before testing what you believe to be the strongest ones in quantitative research—and certainly before assigning the commercial development to your creative people. Yes, it's a multiple-step process. So get your act together and develop a process that can move at the fastest, yet most effective speed possible.

How to find the right benefit? Again, that takes research. Promise testing is one type of benefit testing that we heartily endorse. It not only ranks an array of benefits—the selling promises—but when done right tells you which are the most unique and which have the most leverage in the marketplace.

Just remember that a promise test is not a test of concepts or executions. Just of benefits. Keep them simple, short, and to the point. And be sure to test them with and without the brand name. You'll be amazed at how different the winners may turn out to be.

What is a benefit (promise)? A benefit can be many things:

- a way to respond to peer pressure
- a way to feel better about oneself
- a cry for status
- a better working result (efficacy)

- a more satisfying feel or look
- faster service

And the list goes on and on . . .

Most promise tests that we've been involved with have at least ten promises that are tested and another twenty or so that just didn't make the final cut. It's not easy work to get everyone to agree as to what the benefits could or should be, but it's all worth it in the end.

And remember that consumer benefits will logically change as you narrow the market segment you're selling to. The key is to match the one(s) with the most leverage to the target audience that will generate actual buying with an affordable level of marketing.

When the testing is over and your marketing team has agreed on the promise to be advertised, don't just sell it; sell it HARD. Repeat the promise over and over again. Get it known, understood, and part of the culture of the target audience that you are selling to.

For those of you who have seen the DVD of the Clark Gable film *The Hucksters,* you'll get the reference: "Beautee Soap! Beautee Soap! Beautee Soap!" For those of you who've never seen it, it's a great rental that can teach us all something about advertising selling. A hard sell doesn't have to involve mindlessly repeating the product name or benefit. It can be a sweet, little old lady saying, "Where's the beef?" or an ex

Presidential contender saying, "It worked for me"—and you've driven home the benefit in a memorable way.

Now imagine (or remember) this: An entire commercial of squares. Square buildings. Square drinking glass coasters. Square sinks. Everything in your life that's square. Then, at the end, the curvaceous lines of the new Volkswagen Beetle.

Repetitive? Yes. Clever? Absolutely. Translates to print? Totally. Single-minded? Yep. Boring and old-fashioned? No way.

In the OTC (over-the-counter nonprescription drug) category we referred to it as "What's the promise? What's the proof?" You're promising someone relief. Are you promising it quickly or long-term? Exclusively or better than the other guy? And then what's the proof you're offering to make the promise believable?

We're not just talking OTC here. Asking yourself "what's our promise and what's our proof?" is as good a way as any at getting a personal handle on your product benefit so you can begin to create. And when you do, put the benefit in the headline. Put it in the last line of copy. Make it the hero of your visual. Leave the viewer with the benefit in your TV commercial, movie commercial, or even corporate video.

Corny? Yes. Old-fashioned? Well, it doesn't have to be, though the idea of it is. Effective? Absolutely. And isn't that the point of your job?

32

Tell 'em, Sell 'em, and Tell 'em Again

NAME FIVE COMMERCIALS YOU SAW LAST NIGHT, ONE BANNER on a Web site you went to today, and the ad on the back cover of the last magazine you read?

Chances are you can't even correctly name one.

Now do you get it?

The average consumer is exposed to about 3,500 ads or commercial messages each day. (We have no idea where that number comes from but it's the one generally used in the industry. Or maybe we just made up that statistic.) The point is neither you nor anyone else can have significant recall of what you've just seen.

Aha, a lightbulb should have just gone off in your head! No wonder these guys keep harping about what works and what doesn't. Right! You can't afford to waste precious seconds of your sales pitch—and one mention of what you're selling isn't enough.

It's repetition, repetition, repetition that makes your advertising memorable and successful. Well, not exactly. Unlike *The Hucksters,* we're not proposing you start pounding "Beautee Soap, Beautee Soap, Beautee Soap." We're talking about the focus of a simple, clear, singular message in your commercial.

How many times have you seen a commercial where they've put everything in except the name of the ad agency? If you're trying to get someone's attention in today's marketplace, you damned well better be sure you're only trying to tell one, clear story.

If you want to learn how to use one key selling message, you don't have to look any further than the tabloid newspapers. To grab and hold a newsstand sale, the editors have to decide what the one, single most important (or attention-getting) story is for the day, then scream it in 96-point type on the front of the paper. And if you want a more exotic education, go to the Plaka in Greece or the Casbah in Marrakech and see how the vendors get and keep your attention with their rudimentary command of English and their brilliant command of what makes a sale.

Tell 'em once. Sell 'em hard with the benefit repeated and then tell 'em you've told them by telling the whole story again. Boring, you say? Well, it's the job of your creative team to make sure that it's not only not boring, but it's fascinating and memorable.

Impossible, you say? No, certainly not impossible. Advertising has worked since the first day a caveman decided to cover up his private parts instead of letting them hang out. (Mystery! Intrigue! Allure!) But it *is* hard work and it's getting harder to do effectively.

The tell 'em, sell 'em, and tell 'em again scenario is a philosophy that should be discussed between advertiser and advertising agency well before work begins on any campaign. It's one of the basic ground rules that should be put into play before advertising is presented to the client for approval. What it means is that the marketing people and creative people have to agree on what the one, clear message will be. And the client has to agree to use that one, clear message across all their advertising.

It's tempting to put every single "reason to believe" in a strategy brief. But they should all be secondary to the one, focused, key selling message. Then, if the campaign doesn't deliver that one clear message, it shouldn't be approved.

Good luck, success, and may the gods be with you. Whichever gods you believe in.

33
Tell 'em Who Told 'em

THIRTY YEARS AGO TV COMMERCIALS RAN IN A RELATIVELY uncluttered environment. Sixty-second spots weren't overly rare, competitive commercials didn't run in the same pod, there were far fewer commercials every hour. Today you don't have the luxury of assuming viewers will watch your commercial or sit through the whole thing to catch your name at the end.

Here are several tips that we know work, time and time again. You won't want to do all of them in the same commercial, but you just might want to do more than one if you're serious about creating brand awareness.

- Put a bug in the lower right hand corner. You know what a bug is, right? That's the television industry term for the annoying graphic that often appears in the lower right hand corner and lets you know what network you're watching. Ignore your creative people who'll scream that it's "mussing up" the commercial message. It isn't. We're all now trained to see lots of things on the screen at the same time and still pay attention to the message.

- Get your brand name or a logo design seen early in the commercial via some kind of graphic essential to the commercial message. Or, design a logo or editorial treatment of your brand that's memorable. As we said earlier in the book, Leo Burnett created some of the world's most effective advertising using icons. Charlie the Tuna. The Maytag Repairman. The Jolly Green Giant. The Marlboro Man. The entire commercial was the company logo. Brilliant!
- Whether you're using a voice-over or on-screen talent, have your brand mentioned at least two times in the commercial.
- Always, always end your commercial with your brand name prominently on the screen.

Obvious? Maybe so. But obviously overlooked far too often. You've got to do what one of our bosses used to call "Mr. Potatohead." You have to learn to lean back, squint your eyes, pretend you've never seen the commercial before, and then ask yourself, "Will my message get through to someone who's only going to see this once?"

Go ahead, start squinting.

34

The Younger the Audience, the More Cuts You Can Use

AN UPCOMING TIP IS ABOUT TALKING TO YOUR CUSTOMERS IN their own language (Tip #37). Commercial editing is one of those languages.

We referred to it earlier as "GenY velocity." Younger audiences can handle more scenes, edits, and cuts in their commercials than older audiences can.

We're trained to see and process things the way we learned as children. We're talking here about how the brain is wired, folks. It's almost asking the impossible of older audiences to follow the pace of a spot that younger audiences easily understand.

For example, watch a sports program with someone in their eighties. If there are other things going on in the room (diverging conversations, chatter, small talk), you'll find the older person is confused, time and again, by instant replay. It's not Alzheimer's, it's just how their brains were wired. They grew up in a world without instant reply and it's difficult to process replays, cuts, and slo-mo graphics.

Same is true for print: younger audiences have been trained to process images on a page differently than older audiences can.

Don't just get sucked into the style and rhythm of your editors, producers, and directors. For the most part they'll want to be young, hip, and contemporary. Fine. Good for them. But that might not be how best to communicate to your audience.

As you look at the rough edit of your commercial, ask yourself, "Who am I talking to?" Depending on the age answer you get, make sure you pace the spot accordingly.

Of course if you're talking to a younger audience who'll respond to the contemporary style, then let the people you hired do their jobs (Tip #49). Trust your editor, producer, and director and let them deliver a high-energy, hot, music-video style commercial that speaks directly to your target audience. If you're not the target audience and the edit makes you uncomfortable, that's a good sign. Just make sure the discomfort is due to the editorial style and not some fundamental flaw in the actual message.

Now go and cut away to your heart's content.

35

Create Advertising That Gets Talked About or Used in Everyday Conversation

"CAN YOU HEAR ME NOW?"

"Where's the beef?"

"Try it, you'll like it."

"I can't believe I ate the whole thing."

"What's the story?"

Depending on how old you are, you'll know anywhere from one to all of those lines. If you're under thirty, chances are you know all those lines—but didn't know they came from TV commercials.

It's called "stickiness." And if you haven't read it yet, here's an unsolicited endorsement for Malcolm Gladwell's brilliant marketing book *The Tipping Point*.

Whether it's the opening four notes of Beethoven's Fifth Symphony, a hip-hop lyric that rattles around in your head, or a commercial line that moves into pop culture conversation, the goal is the same: stickiness.

How do you get it? A lot of work, serious talent, and a little bit of luck. Stickiness comes in three ways: execution, repetition, and zeitgeist.

Execution: Unique casting, a quirky line reading, a little magic on the set—all of these can combine to catch the public's attention and imagination.

Repetition: The sheer weight of your media buy could drive home the point. For years, Procter & Gamble's Mr. Whipple told us "please don't squeeze the Charmin." Problem was, people remembered—and wished they didn't. Stickiness should, ideally, involve something you actually want to have stick.

Zeitgeist: Capturing the temper or mood of the time at just the right moment. When Verizon Wireless went with "can you hear me now?," they turned a phrase of frustration (dropout calls on your cell phone) into a positive—and rode the wave of the public's reaction.

Now here's the bad news: there's no accounting for taste. You can do everything we suggested above and . . . zippo. Nada. Nothing. Like your commercial disappeared in the void. That's the luck part. Sorry. If there were a guaranteed way to create memorable advertising, our industry would be far more highly valued than it currently is.

PRINT ADVERTISING

"Come get in bed, Harold, and let's read the perfume ads."

Forty years ago Marshall McCluhan announced, "Print is dead"—and then he wrote ten books to prove his point.

The way people process media is changing. That's not good or bad, it's a fact. About 400 years ago, a bunch of concerned parents probably met on a regular basis to fret about the new thing all their kids were doing:

"Reading?" they worried. "If all they're going to do is read books, how will they memorize anything?"

Magazine and newspaper articles are getting shorter. Attention spans are decreasing. But check out the newsstands, they're packed with new and ever more content related to today's lifestyles.

And log on to the Internet—any site, any day, anyplace in the world. No matter how many video clips or Flash animations they show you, ultimately they expect you to read. The Internet (in case you didn't know it) is just print delivered on a different platform. So when we talk about "print," we're talking about the Internet as well. Print is still an effective way to reach and speak to your audience. Just make sure you speak to them in ways that deliver your message.

36

Don't Hide Your Brand Name

WHASSAMATTA? NOT PROUD OF YOUR COMPANY, YOUR CLIENT'S company or brand? Grow up. Your job is to get that brand noticed somehow, anyhow! Noticed, recognized, admired, and wanted.

When we talked about television, we talked about getting your brand name on the screen as much as possible, at a minimum twice. The same is true for print. Great advertising should catch the viewer's interest and shout who you are. In the average print vehicle your ad is competing with at least fifty or more other advertisements—never mind the editorial content and whatever else is happening to the reader in this multitasking world.

Screaming your brand name is especially true when your brand or company name shows up on a Google search list.

You need to do everything you can to get your brand to stand out and get remembered. What's the single best way? Put your brand name in the headline or at least in the subhead.

More room.
Free drinks.
Less explaining yourself to accounting.
The world's most affordable Business Class

Not a bad headline and subhead.

> **More room.**
> **Free drinks.**
> **Less explaining yourself to accounting.**
> **airTran. The world's most affordable Business Class**

Add the brand name airTran. Same thought, equally poor use of periods and spacing, but at least the second version gives the advertiser a better chance of being remembered—especially if they're not going to read the copy or glance down for the logo.

"Make the logo bigger" is one of the classic pejorative advertising stereotypes. Designers and art directors always take that remark as proof that the client has no taste and no sense of design. Perhaps. But so what? Don't be so literal. Recognize that "make the logo bigger" often means make it easier for the reader or viewer to figure out who's talking to them. Makes great sense.

Where should the logo be? The old rule is still the right rule: the lower-right-hand corner. Another essential. But we often find that even ads with the logo in the right place have it in a type size too small to get attention from most browsers.

Think about it another way. Would you ever send out a résumé without your name on the top or have a business card with your name in a hard-to-read place in a hard-to-read typeface? Never waste an opportunity to get the brand name noticed.

And maybe it's not just a logo. Maybe it's also a mnemonic device, like an 800 number. Be creative. Use every tool at your disposal.

No matter how good your advertising is, no matter how creative the work is, no matter how coordinated all your messages are, there are always obtrusive and unobtrusive opportunities to register the brand name. Use them.

Don't waste brand opportunities. Hell, if the only thing that anyone ever remembers about your ad or commercial is the brand name, at least they've gotten that. It's a lot better than remembering the joke or even the benefit but not having a clue whose product delivers the benefit.

So be proud of your brand name. Use it often. Make it integral to the selling idea. The easier it is to remember your name, the faster they'll remember it. Or as media guru Gene DeWitt likes to say: "Anyone can get noticed by spending $200 million. The skill is getting noticed if you're spending $10 million."

37

Talk to Your Customers in Their Own Language

"IT BEHOOVES YOU TO ARTICULATE YOUR MESSAGE IN A MANner with which your end user can identify." (College professor)

"'Sup?" (Urban teenager)

"I mean like, whatever." (Teenage girl)

Get the point? Essentially the same thought written three different ways to three different audiences.

Who are you talking to? How are you talking to them? Yes, it's grammatically correct to say, "Whom are you talking to?" but advertising is the spoken word in print. Which is a key point worth repeating:

ADVERTISING IS THE SPOKEN WORD IN PRINT

We all like to be with and buy things from people who are like us and whom we like. It's human nature. So when selling, it's essential to know who you're talking to and to understand how and why you're talking to them as you are.

Think about talking and listening to people you like and don't like. Think of some of the dates you've gone on. Do you know that if you don't like someone's cadence and manner of speaking you'll never enter a serious relationship with that person? True.

Great advertising seeks a relationship. It should speak one-to-one. Emotionally, it's about one person putting his arm around the shoulder of a friend and saying, "Hey, I know you've got a problem or need. Well, I've got a solution that's just right for you."

We mentioned the late, great Leo Burnett. The second President Bush was also a master of knowing his customer's voice. No fast-talking glib Easterner, he. In fact the Republican party goes to great lengths to get its message in exactly the right voice. They have successfully defined the political agenda with language.

Gearheads want to learn from gearheads, stock traders want to hear from someone who speaks Wall Street jargon. It's not wrong; it's just the way we relate. The rhythms, idioms, and syntax of your writing should match what your audience is most comfortable with. Can it be done? Yes. Is it really hard? No.

In one of our workshops we ask the participants to read one of several one- or two-page writings we hand out. We then ask them to *hand-copy* the first paragraph of what they've read and then immediately write a description of a person they know. In almost every case, what they write about the person tends to be in the general style of what they've just read. It's a fascinating phenomenon and there's a term for it: modeling.

If you have to write to a particular audience, start each day by typing something in the language of that audience. You start to build up an internal sense of the rhythm of their speech. And in a short while, you're writing the way they talk.

What do you think Tiger Woods does on his days off? It's called practice. Do it. The people you want to reach want to feel that you understand them. Your language tells them you do. Or, don't. Today, how you speak to someone is as important as what you have to say.

It used to be that an agency would hire a specialist to write for a client. "He's a car guy" or "he's a drug guy" were common phrases. (In the 1960s, "he's a drug guy" had a different meaning, but that's another story.) There was a reason those guys got and demanded top dollar. They knew their clients, the client's products, and their audiences, and they could communicate to those audiences in perfect pitch and tone. They had that language down to a virtual science.

Voice is another reason there's a paucity of long copy advertisements in today's world: there's a lack of knowledge and understanding of how to communicate to one's audience brilliantly. If you don't know, you can't write successfully. So how do you stay on top of an evolving language? Read what your customers read, watch what they watch (Tip #3).

If you've got to talk to teens, read their magazines. Watch the TV shows they're tuning in to. Go to the movies they're watching. The chat rooms they're in. Learn the language of e-mail. Do the same for kids, men, women, and young adults. By tuning in to their media, you'll learn what's important to them—and how they're talking about it. Equally important, you'll start to understand in what medium they're talking to each other.

Read, study, learn "voice." Become a specialist. Sell. You'll get top billing and big bucks.

38

Put a Benefit in the Headline

YOU MIGHT THINK THIS IS A DUPLICATE OF EVERY OTHER point we've made regarding selling the benefit, and *you're right*. And because it's such an important point we not only repeated it but we've put it in our headline.

Get the prospect's attention by telling him what he wants to know immediately. Don't make him guess your brand's benefit. Don't make fun of the brand and the benefit. Don't make fun of his needing the brand and the benefit. Make sure you know the difference between making fun and having fun.

For instance, GenY humor is sarcastic, droll, and sometimes caustic. It can work in a commercial and can successfully be used to market your product. But if you use it, make sure your creative people have used it in the right direction: make sure they're having fun *with* the product (maybe at the expense of others). Making fun *of* the product (or its users) is a sure way to kill it.

Asking yourself "What's our promise and what's our proof?" is as good a way as any at getting a personal handle on your product benefit so you can begin to create.

What are you promising your customer? Will you make their life easier? Make them smarter? Make their company more efficient? Well, don't make them figure that out. Tell them, as quickly and clearly as possible, what they'll get out of your product or service.

Okay, we hear some of you saying "I don't think the ads I see are so bad." If that's the case, you're just not reading enough magazines.

Time and time again we need to actually search through ads to find one that's good. But Jeff just found one so bad that he demands time to list its faults.

The ad is by a savvy and successful stock brokerage firm. Its management needs to be thankful that its success is not dependent on the ad they ran in *Forbes* magazine.

1. It has no headline.
2. There's no benefit in the ad.
3. The visual is more than boring (just a profile of a beyond-middle-aged man).
4. The ad has forty-one words in it, but the amazing thing is that twenty-seven of them are virtually unreadable.
   a. They're in tiny type.
   b. They're in white on a black background (reverse type).
   c. They're positioned vertically down the middle of the page next to the profile.
   d. They're not even in a straight line but rather curve around the profile.

Zounds! (That's Jeff being astonished. Steve thought he should go with Egads! Or Yowie!) Totally unreadable. What a waste of money. Jeff actually showed the ad to an ex–marketing executive, who was astounded and embarrassed.

Why do so many people get it wrong when it just isn't that hard to do what's right? Figure out why people would really benefit from your product or service. Then tell 'em. Make it interesting. Make it readable. It's that easy—but for some, apparently, it's that hard.

39
White Space Is Valuable

See? We got your attention.

40

Long Copy Can Sell

NOBODY READS ANYMORE. CERTAINLY NOBODY READS BODY copy in an ad. Lies, lies, and more lies.

You're still reading this book. Why? Because you think there's something of value here for you. You see a benefit in getting the information that's contained here. ("Again with the benefit," you ask? Duh.)

There's no rational reason to create billboard-type advertising in media other than billboards. Unless the creative team just doesn't want to work very hard. Or they have a stupendous idea that really works in six words or less.

If you're selling an image, then use an image. Long copy isn't needed when a picture can tell a thousand words. And we're not advocating the continual use of long-copy ads. We're just saying borrow a page from your Internet site and bring it over to print. People go to the Internet for information. They want to know about a product or service. Why? Because they're not getting that information in the advertising. So why make the sale a two-step process? If it's important to put the information in the ad, put it in the ad. If all you want to communicate is style, then shorter is better.

Prospects do read long copy, especially "about-to-buy"

prospects in the market for a considered purchase such as a car, a financial product, or a capital expenditure for a business.

Most buyers about to shell out big bucks want to know as much as they can about the product and brand they're buying. These prospects become "mavens" (Yiddish for experts) in the category. Help them if you want to sell to them.

Mavens and "about-to-buys" are constantly on the search for benefits they would like, features they are interested in, and how your brand builds its competitive edge over the competition. The more you tell them, the more they'll know. Again, this is why the Internet has become so valuable to buyers. The Internet lets the buyers do the research they can basically no longer do in print advertising.

And once these more knowledgeable consumers make up their mind, they will unquestionably repeat the benefits and features to everyone who will listen to them. They will not only become buyers but great salespeople for your brand.

Never be afraid of long copy. Long copy can and likely will:

1. separate your brand from the competition
2. provide your brand with a perceived level of expertise
3. generate high awareness scores in the publications in which it runs

4. increase the "intent-to-buy" scores of even those not in the "about-to-buy" segment

5. provide information for the people other people turn to for advice

One caveat about long copy: it's getting harder and harder to find an art director who really knows how to design a long copy ad and has the patience to design it so it is at its most readable. (If you find one, hire him; he'll be worth his weight in gold.) And we mean an art director, not a designer. What's the difference? Glad you asked us that. What's the difference between a poster and an ad? Designers do posters. They're glamorous, stylish, contemporary art pieces featuring a commercial product. Some of the greatest poster art of the 1920s and 1930s are priceless artworks today. An art director is a person who can use her artistic skills to direct the visual communication. They're both valuable skills, but we'll take an art director over a designer any day of the week.

An art director understands the hierarchy of messaging and makes sure your eye goes to each key point in the order it's supposed to go. Designing a long-copy ad takes care and exacting work. It also takes terrific teamwork between the art director and the copywriter. Some critical points to spend time on are:

- typeface selection (Make it readable. Use a serif typeface.)

- headline and subhead design (Be specific and say what you have to say to draw the reader into the body copy.)
- paragraph length (Use short sentences and paragraphs.)
- body copy headings (Use them frequently. Keep them short with lots of white space around them.)
- column width (Maximize white space and keep the columns a size that makes the ad easy to read.)
- white space (If at all possible don't use the bleed space on a page. The wider the border the better.)
- readable copy (Never use reverse type in the body copy.)

And finally, when the ad has been written, designed, and approved, let it "ripen" for a day or two and then come back for final edits and approval. You'll be glad you did.

Oh, another final point—see if you can use the ad in your blog, your Web site, and your point-of-sale literature. We'll bet you can and that it will do double duty for you and your brand. That's a great money saver and revenue producer.

Have we said enough? We could keep going—and we bet you'd continue to read.

41

Know When and How to Scream **SALE!**

SALE! DON'T EVER HIDE THAT WORD. SOME PEOPLE SAY IT'S the most powerful word in the English language. We're not sure about that, but it's definitely in our Top 10.

If you're seeking sales in the next day or week, then run an ad that says it. And if at all possible, promote the price and the savings. Sale advertising works, sale advertising with specifics works even better—as long as you use it sparingly over time.

Jeff has a garden nursery near his home that has a front sign that says "50% OFF." The sign has been there for a full year. Do you think anyone who has driven by and seen that sign over the year now really believes that sale? No way.

Before you think about running a sale, ask yourself a key question: why?

If you're trying to clear out inventory, that's one purpose. If you're trying to make your Wall Street numbers for the quarter, that's another. If you're trying to increase market share over the long term by taking a short-term profit hit, that's a third. Knowing why you want to run a sale will guide you to the most effective message.

There's an old rule in advertising: live by price, die by price. Crazy who? Jerry who? Nobody beats who? Dennison

Clothiers? If you're under thirty, you don't even know what we're talking about. These were all practically household expressions, coined by advertisers who promoted their price, and price alone. While they say "advertising has no memory," a better homily might be "smart advertisers have long memories." It's helpful to remember the failures—they'll keep you from making similar mistakes with your own brand.

If your entire brand image is built around low price, you better make a lot of money and sell out in a hurry. Because one day, sooner or later, someone's going to figure out how to make and sell what you do for less. (Think China.) And when they do, your customers will leave you as fast as they came.

One of the chief values of a sale is surprise. When consumers expect you to cut your price, you've lost a key value component. So if seasonal demands mean people are looking for your sale, then find a new way to say it. Of course it's the same sale you've had every year; but with a fresh spin, you can reinvigorate your efforts and make the expected unexpected.

Sale advertising has a place in your mix, but it's got to be part of that mix, not a separate element. Never run a one-time schlock sales ad unless you're willing to see your brand suffer. Every ad is an investment in the brand image.

And never let a retailer run a schlock ad for your brand, either. Don't abdicate your brand stewardship to another company. Besides preparing dealer ads, you should make it a rule that all local and dealer advertising must be approved by your company.

Study the advertising of those who run sale ads all the time: the automobile manufacturers and big retailers. They've trained the consumer to only buy at sale prices. (Rebates, employee pricing.) Don't make the same mistake. On the other hand, those guys know how to scream sale. Learn the good from them as well as the bad.

Don't be bashful about running an end-of-year or end-of-model sale. Consumers are smart enough to recognize that they can be great deals and they can even make your brand more valuable if the new model is superior to the old. (It should be. If it isn't, why not?) Use "same time next year" sales sparingly unless there's an industry mantra that's so powerful you can't break it. (President's Day car sales.) Try selling cars the week before the sale. You can't (unless the price is slashed) because smart consumers will wait until the sale is advertised—it's only days away.

Sale advertising is essential for most brands and it's powerful. Use it judiciously and it can help build your brand, build your share, or make your numbers. Use it poorly and it can destroy your brand. Sometimes in a matter of months.

THE INTERNET

"This 'digital revolution'—can we muscle in on that?"

*A*in't technology swell. Just when you thought you'd mastered the marketing complexities of television, cable, satellite TV, spot TV, spot cable, and direct response, along comes this pesky thing called the Internet. And even if you wanted to ignore it five years ago, you're shit out of luck. It's here—and it's only going to grow in importance. First there was dealing with your own site. Now there's dealing with Web advertising. And blogs and podcasts are here—yours, your competitors', and your consumers'. Now the hot trend is communities. And by the time this book gets published you'll probably have some new variations to deal with as well.

Well, the tips are good no matter what the medium—it's all about communications. And we've got a couple of things to say about this newest frontier of all.

42

Make the Navigation to Your Selling Page as Easy as Possible

THE INTERNET IS AN ADVERTISER'S DREAM. YOU NOT ONLY target the sale incredibly efficiently, you can actually make the sale right there, right then! And if you've done everything right, the prospect has shown up *because they're actually hunting for your product, your brand! Yippee!*

Now the bad news: Advertising on the Internet is more challenging because it's new, different, and still evolving. First you could get away with banners. Then those got ignored. Next came pop-ups. Now those are being filtered. Now there are links, premium and paid.

Notice how every piece of good news seems to be followed by a bad news paragraph? Well, that's the good news—and the bad news. It's not what you know, it's knowing what to do with what you know that matters. That's what the bad news is usually about—showing you how to put what you know to good use.

TV is about entertainment, the Internet is about information. People seek it out. They're looking for pricing. They're looking for specifications. They're looking for examples of what you've done. When you've got someone on your site, there's no such thing as too much information. The key is to deliver that information in a usable form. Most of what we've offered in terms of gaining awareness, interest, and re-call holds for all Internet advertising. But one issue really stands out once you've gotten that A.I.R.—closing the sale.

Most potential online sales are lost before the final OK is clicked. If you get them that far in the first place.

Web site navigation is the number-one key ingredient in making the sale. If people can't find what they want quickly and easily (and feel it's foolproof and secure), they're going to go somewhere else to get the information (and buy the product).

So how do you improve the odds of making a sale?

- Eliminate any pages or instructions that will confuse and frustrate the user.
- Keep all instructions consistent in tone.
- Keep all page formats, especially the customer data pages, consistent in format.
- Make finding forgotten passwords easy to recover—but secure!
- Keep the action buttons—Continue, Accept, OK, Next Step—in the same place on every page. And make them big and easy to find.
- Learn from the best. Buy items from several different Web vendors and then use the best pages from the process to build or edit your site.

- Always make it easy for the user to retrace her steps. Let the Back button do its job.
- When the user commits an error, make sure the correction instructions are crystal clear. Never embarrass the user.
- Don't put too much information on any page. (Remember the concept of white space. It works on the Web also. In fact, as we write this there's a big debate about the uncluttered Google opening page versus the cluttered Yahoo opening page. The critics are on the side of Google. Will the facts and opinions stay consistent very long? We doubt it.)
- Always measure your customer's performance. The Web is the ultimate medium for testing. Take advantage of that.
  - Make sure your objectives are being met.
  - Know what your competition is doing and compare and react.
  - Maintain an ongoing tracking of your Web site performance. Keep it on an improving curve.

Before you start to design or redesign your Web site, visit a half-dozen competitors'. Make a note of what you like and dislike—first impressions! Try to buy something from them.

Go to a search engine and type in your product or brand

or company name. See where you show up on the engine. If you're not on page one, you're in big trouble. Are your competitors listed before you?

And what about your retailers? Where do they fit in? Are your products being given proper space on their sites? Are you preparing "Web mats" they can drop in that add more sizzle to your product on their sites? (The answer should be "yes.")

Don't let your IT people or Web designers bamboozle you with talk about how hard something is (Tip #28). Gleefully admit you're a complete idiot and then cheerfully remind them that you're paying the bills, and until you understand exactly what they're suggesting (and exactly why they're suggesting it) there's no way you're paying for anything. Remember you're not alone in being frustrated by expensive, confusing IT that doesn't work. Then cut them a little slack and teach them a thing or two about marketing so they get it right the first time.

There's lots of learning to be done with Web advertising. Give it the resources and time that it demands and deserves. And make sure the people designing, building, and maintaining your site give *you* the resources and time *you* demand and deserve.

43

Blogs—Still Lots of Learning to be Done

OKAY, YOU CAUGHT US. WHEN IT COMES TO BLOGS, WE CER-
tainly can't claim this is inside-the-box thinking. It's too early
to have anything except out-of-the-box thinking. But we do
have some suggestions.

1. Know your target audience. Don't try to be all for all.
2. Keep your communication clear and concise.
3. No hype. Tell it like it is. Hype will read dishonest to
   a substantial number of readers. Don't get trashed
   because of overexuberance.
4. Tell the truth or don't write anything. Even a white
   lie will backfire every time, when virtually anybody
   and everybody is a knowledgeable critic with world-
   wide exposure.
5. Answer all comments as quickly as possible. The
   good, the bad, the ugly; but especially the bad and
   the ugly.
6. Be upfront about who your sponsor/investor is. Your
   reputation and the reputation of your sponsor are
   at risk.
7. Keep your eyes and ears open in the world of blog-

ging. It is changing and will continue to change at a breakneck pace.

8. Good luck!

"What?" you ask. "You're saying my company should have a blog?" Absolutely. And it can either be under your name or anonymous. Blogs are your opportunity to speak directly to your customers and let them speak directly to you. Think of them as your own, private, paid-for-by-the-consumer focus group. It's a place you can get feedback that can improve your products and refine your sales techniques. Managed properly, a blog can be an invaluable resource for tracking trends.

At the same time, you should be monitoring other people's blogs as well. There are new companies starting up that can (as of this writing) track the 16+ million blog sites for any mention of your products or services (and your competitors' as well).

We advocate signing up and seeing what people are saying when they think you're not listening. Just as there are Early Adaptors who spread glowing words about a company, there are now Early Detractors who are eager to go on their sites and trash you. You've got to know where the enemy is at all times. The more you know, the easier it is to quash or counter any rumors before they get out of control.

That goes for blogs and communities as well. In a couple of years, there will be communities for everything. Including people who love and people who hate your products and services. Stay on top of it by starting a community of your own. Keep it open and honest. Let complaints as well as compliments pour in. Monitor the community for new product ideas, refinements, and improvements. Use the knowledge you gain from these free-flowing focus groups to stay ahead of the consumer curve.

It takes effort and dedication. We know you can do it.

RADIO, OUTDOOR, AND DIRECT RESPONSE

"Now, that's product placement!"

*T*hree media going through a revolution.

Radio has the power to achieve sales results and market impressions in ways TV no longer can—and at a significant savings in price. But with Sirius, XM, and podcasting, finding your audience is getting as tough as cable TV.

Outdoor can deliver a highly-targeted message literally block-by-block, and you should use it accordingly. The more creative the better. It's really that simple.

Direct response? Direct response television has become a highly specialized art form and should be part of your retail mix. For direct response via snail mail hire the best agency, best list analyst, and test, test, test.

44
Radio:
Tell a Story

PAUL FREES: Radio? Why should I advertise on radio? There's nothing to look at, no pictures . . .

STAN FREBERG: Look, you can do things on radio you couldn't possibly do on TV.

FREES: That'll be the day.

FREBERG: All right, watch this . . . ahem, okay people, now when I give you the cue, I want the 700-foot mountain of whipped cream to roll into Lake Michigan, which has been drained and filled with hot chocolate. Then the Royal Canadian Air Force will fly overhead towing a 10-ton maraschino cherry, which will be dropped into the whipped cream to the cheering of 25,000 extras. All right—cut the mountain!

(Appropriate SFX)

Cue the Air Force!

(Appropriate SFX)

Cue the maraschino cherry!

(Appropriate SFX)

Okay, 25,000 cheering extras!

(Appropriate SFX, which end abruptly)

Now, you want to try that on television?

FREES: Well . . .

FREBERG: You see, radio is a very special medium, because it stretches the imagination.

FREES: But doesn't television stretch the imagination?

FREBERG: Up to 27 inches, yes.

Well, now we're up to about 64 inches . . . but you get the picture! That's a thirty-year-old radio commercial. It's as powerful, funny, and relevant today as it was when the late, great Stan Freberg first wrote it for the National Association of Broadcasters. It's the only complete example we have in this entire book, but it's worth including because it tells you everything you want to know about radio.

Here's what you need to know about radio advertising:

1. You've got time. You've got 30 or 60 or even 120 seconds to tell your story. You can do justice to your product or service and you'll have the room you need to do it right. The decision to go to fifteen-second selling units for TV was a budget decision, not a marketing decision. Given more time, you just might have a better chance of making a sale. Radio gives you more time.

2. You've got a good chance to capture the listener's attention. People generally listen to radio in their cars. They listen to radio alone. In short, you've got a captive audience. Take advantage of it. Play with them. Get them emotionally involved in your story. Get them to stop multitasking for a minute.

3. You can really grab the listener's imagination. Freberg's spot is a brilliant example of what you can do on radio. With sound effects and editing you can bring in a cast of thousands . . . fly in the entire Royal Canadian Air Force . . . invade a country . . . travel to other planets. . . . You're only limited by *your* imagination, not the listener's.

Radio is a highly creative medium that's generally overlooked for reasons we'll discuss shortly. Step up. Be the first on your block to take advantage of the fact that your competitors aren't there. We think the General Motors OnStar commercials are a powerful example of using this medium effectively. Talk about giving listeners a direct experience of the product! Yes, they've moved the campaign over to television— but if you notice, the television commercials are just the radio spots. There's (literally) no picture. It's just the actual sounds of actual people calling the OnStar help line. Which is what makes the radio so effective: they use the full sixty seconds to let the real-life drama unfold.

Believe us when we say that radio isn't just for local retail mattress companies or herbal cures. The right spot in the right daypart can add significant impact to your bottom line.

The people who put together recommendations for you don't like to recommend radio. Why?

1. It ain't sexy. When creative people go on job interviews, they bring their print and their on-air reels. They don't think they're going to get a higher-paying job by playing radio commercials. They don't have spots like the one above on their reel, if they even have a reel.

2. It ain't glamorous. Nobody gets to fly off to Majorca to record a radio spot. (Except, perhaps, the ad agency for the Majorca Tourist Bureau.) If the client wants a radio spot it usually means walking over to the nearby recording studio and working in a tiny, windowless room.

3. It ain't profitable. Radio commercials cost less to produce. Radio commercials cost less to run. So the media company and ad agency don't make as much money selling you radio. Which means you now know what they're selling you.

So when your media people come by to give you next year's recommendations, you might want to ask them "where's the radio?" And if they give you all these answers that sound like a poor excuse, walk them down to their cars, make them turn on the power, and see what station(s) all their radios are tuned to. Then send them back to their offices to redo their plans.

45

Outdoor: Make It Simple, Big, and Memorable

USE NINE WORDS (OR FEWER) WITH A GREAT VISUAL. (This is one of the few places Jeff and Steve disagreed in the book. Jeff says: "nine words or fewer." Steve says: "Three words, maybe six.")

Okay, want more information than that? Here it is:

KEEP IT BIG.

KEEP IT SIMPLE.

MAKE IT MEMORABLE.

Picture this: you're cruising down the highway at 70+ miles per hour looking for openings in the traffic and cops around the curve. Then off to the right there's a billboard. And on it, in unreadable type, is an ad for a product or company and you can barely make out the . . . oh shit, there's the cop.

Big. Simple. Memorable. The three key points for creating great outdoor advertising. If you can accomplish all three, you're a hero. All you need to do is get in your car and drive a few miles, see the trash that's been created, approved, and hung and you'll see just how heroic you can be.

Outdoor is generally a blight on advertising as well as the environment. But it doesn't need to be either. Here are some of the key thoughts that need to be remembered as you create heroic outdoor advertising:

- It will likely be read in a moving car—with the radio on and possibly a cell phone conversation in progress. In other words, you don't have your audience's undivided attention. If, in fact, you have any attention at all.
- The driver is not generally expecting the billboard so he's not looking for it. Think of it as a drive-by pop-up window.
- What works on an 8-by-10-inch layout probably will not work when the billboard is 80 by 100 feet and 300 feet off the roadway. Think scale from the very beginning: don't try to scale up after the work is created.

By now you get it: you've got to grab their attention and understanding in a hurry.

This is truly the place where a picture is worth a thousand words. Because if you've got 1,000 words, no one will read them. Except on the billboards approaching the Lincoln Tunnel in rush hour. Those advertisers could do a public service and put up weekly installments of *A Tale of Two Cities* so commuters will have something to do on their wait to work.

The rules are generally inviolate in creating great outdoor advertisements:

1. Never use more than nine words. One to six words are ideal.

2. Keep the type size bigger than you ever would have thought necessary.
3. Create a visual as simple as the words.
4. The visual and the words should "read" as one element to the mind. They must relate.

Outdoor has always demanded that you say it short and sweet. And in today's high-energy multitasking universe, just about everything you do has to be done short and sweet—from TV to Web to outdoor and more. Which is why when we're working on a major campaign with radio, TV, Web, and outdoor components, we try to do the outdoor first: if you can get the message right with one key visual and six words or less, then the other elements of the campaign are easy!

Other thoughts?

Always take advantage of the location. Billboards are *site specific*. The value of a billboard isn't just its size, it's the location. The more traffic (vehicular or pedestrian) that can see it, the more it costs. So almost all billboards should integrate the location with the message. A billboard in LA should be different from one in New York. Ditto Maine and Florida. Ditto by neighborhood. Given geographic mapping and databases you should be able to take advantage of segmentation unlike ever before. Based on where the billboard(s) are located, create a message that matches the location—maybe even a delicious nose-thumbing site directly across from your competitors' home offices.

Humor works. If done well, it will extend your advertising as it gets remembered and talked about. By all means take the opportunity to make your audience feel a little bit better because in today's hectic world you'll likely find the driver hassled and unhappy. It always pays to make people smile because they'll like you.

If you want your audience to remember a Web site address or phone number, make them big and an integral part of the message. For example, 1-800 BUYFISH is infinitely more memorable than 1-800-289-3474.

And what about your trucks, vans, and company cars? Read any good trucks lately? Just as we're all familiar with the "how am I driving?" sign on the back of trucks, these rolling billboards are grossly underutilized. Think about ways you could paint your own trucks (especially the rear doors of the trailer). Or, even more fun, buy the space from a trucker to do a rolling promotion.

A white background makes the billboard more readable at night. Literal white space (which we talked about in print advertising) is truly valuable in outdoor advertising.

Problem/solution advertising works incredibly well in outdoor because it does read so fast. If you can define the problem in a single word, the takeaway of the benefit can be immediate. For instance: "Hungry?" can be a great start to a billboard for fast food advertising on a lonely highway.

And when we say "billboard" or "outdoor," don't just

think of those obnoxious rectangles alongside the interstates. We're really talking "out of home," here. Anyplace your customers might be where they can see your message. With a little creative imagination, you can find new ways to get your message across. Example? ABC premiered the TV series *Desperate Housewives* with clever advertising on dry cleaner plastic garment bags. You know those flimsy, clear plastic wraps they put your clothes in? ABC turned them into clever "billboards" announcing another person who was picking up their dirty laundry. Clever—and the right message for the medium.

So how do you know your billboard will be read? Two ways:

When you think you've got the design you want (or when your agency presents the idea they like), use the technique eye doctors use and make sure you see it the first time in scale.

Before they show you the billboard, have them hold it in scale as far away (and above you) as it will be in real life. So if the billboard's going to be 10 feet tall by 20 feet long, make the comp 10 inches tall by 20 inches long. And if the billboard location is 100 feet from the street, make them hold the layout at least 8½ feet away from you and in the same relative position.

Then—and only then—read the billboard.

The other way is even better: get a digital shot of the actual billboard location and have your creative people comp up the billboard into the photograph taken from street level.

That way, you'll get to see it exactly the way the public will. If you have to think or squint, it's not going to work in real life. Which is the only place that matters.

Make sure your billboard is placed properly. It's essential to have your media buyer "drive the boards" to assess proper placement. Hard-to-see is as common a problem as poor creative.

And finally, never be obtuse with a teaser campaign unless you have oodles and oodles of money. Billboards that try to make you think or anticipate just don't make it in this world of multitasking.

46

Direct Response: Get the List Right

WHO ARE YOU TALKING TO? WHEN IT COMES TO DIRECT RE-sponse, that question is more critical than for any other medium. The single most important element of direct response advertising is your mailing or distribution list. Get it right and you're well on your way to success. Get it wrong and you can wander in the DR universe forever.

Why is the list so important? Common sense affirms the saying "The hungry man sees every bakery on the block." You want to advertise to "interesteds." And you want to advertise to people who are comfortable buying without going to the store.

We're talking direct response and mailing lists—but it's the same as talking network TV and demographics, or maga-zines and readers. Finding your audience is the single most important factor in reaching them. Good media planning and buying will find you an audience. Great media planning and buying will find your audience in places none of your com-petitors are looking (Tip #23).

While Internet shopping continues to grow exponen-tially, there'll always be a role for DR in your mix. Even people who shop or order online prefer the option of browsing a catalog in bed or while watching TV. Get the right message in front of the right audience and you'll have time to make a sale.

How do you find them? This is one of the areas in advertising and marketing where specific expertise is critical. Even if you're a mom-and-pop operation, you need to work with someone who knows how to analyze the metrics of direct response and can estimate the level of sales expected. That analysis is critical and will significantly determine how much you should pay for the lists that you plan to use. Trust us, working with a pro is money well spent and will save you months of time and prevent the waste of lots of money.

Where to look for lists? There are list brokers, or you might want to go direct to the company whose mailing list you think would be right for you. Or if you're trying direct response TV, a specialty direct response TV agency is the place to start.

Once you start your specific list plans make sure that you use portions of several lists in your mailings. Success in direct response is absolutely dependent upon testing and metrics: intuitive thinking doesn't count for a lot; rather it's all in the numbers.

Using several lists (or actually portions of several lists) helps you know which lists have delivered your customers. Once you know those lists that have the highest success in delivering customers—at a reasonable cost per name—you can begin to expand on the portion of that list that was most successful, dump the list that delivered the worst results, and find new lists to test.

In fact TEST is the mantra of direct response. Test every element against initially estimated results. Then test again at every mailing against the best and latest results.

Once you become comfortable with your list strategy and list tactics (and if your DR is on television, read "network strategy" and "time buying tactics"), you should be working on other key elements in direct response. As you will read in the next chapter, there is a definite ranking of important elements and a definite process in testing them.

47

Test Different Offers Against the Benchmark— One Variable at a Time

YOU CHANGE THE PRODUCT'S COLOR. YOU CHANGE THE PRODUCT's price. You change the TV networks you run the offer on. You change the bonus premium offer. Now what's the size of the captain's waistband?

In direct response advertising, once you stray from the tried and true of past proven efforts, nobody ever really knows what's going to work and what isn't. No matter the media vehicle that delivers the sales message, successful direct response advertising depends on hard grunt work, lots of testing, exacting measurement, and the tenacity to stick to a disciplined mode of operation.

The most successful direct response professionals know that a good number of their efforts just won't deliver the results they planned for. That's why direct response efforts should always test at least two different tactical elements. One element of any effort should be the benchmark that's been established from previous mailings. The other elements should test measurable variables against that successful effort.

In order of importance the tactical elements that should be tested are 1) the list, 2) the offer, 3) the package design, 4) the message delivery system, 5) the message itself. Beyond those elements you are for the most part just futzing around with unimportant variables that will add to costs but not add much to revenue.

So it's important to isolate what you're testing at any given time. The key to building a successful direct response business is to establish a benchmark and then, altering one variable at a time, seek to beat that benchmark. When you do, establish a new benchmark and move on from there. Build on successes, learn from and discard failures, and maintain the discipline it takes to build a long-term business.

We say long-term business because most direct response companies look to the long term. They're seeking a repeat customer who will yield incremental revenue over time. They're seeking to find substantial lifetime revenue and profit streams from as many customers as possible. All that to add up to a critical measurement called the lifetime value of the customer. In fact, establishing the lifetime value of a customer is critical to understanding how big a business one can build through direct response advertising.

Is direct response a denigrated medium? You betcha. Is it effective? You betcha. Should it be in your marketing mix? You betcha.

ON THE SET

"Enough storyboarding. Let's shoot something."

ights! Cameras! Checkbook!

Welcome to the strange, exciting, expensive world of production. Whether it's a sixty-second spot for the Super Bowl, a video commercial for the Internet, a print photographer's studio for a dealer ad, or a radio commercial for drive time, going into production means leaving the familiarity of your office and entering a world where no one even owns a tie.

Everyone is a prima donna. Everyone either ignores you or treats you like an idiot. Everyone forgets who's paying the bills.

It can make you uncomfortable. (Jeff says it should.) It can play on your insecurities. It can also bring out the worst "I'll-show-you-who's-the-boss" attitude.

Cool it. They're children, and must be treated that way. Kindly, gently, and with an avuncular manner. Here are a few tips to getting the most out of the shoot—and keeping everyone (including yourself) under control.

But remember, this isn't easy. It's tough, tough work.

48

Never Leave the Set Until the Shooting Board Has Been Covered

"MAGIC ONLY HAPPENS AFTER THE MUNDANE IS COVERED."

Seems obvious, huh? Not always.

If you like feeling anxious, a commercial shoot is your environment. You're pulled in many directions. There's a lot of money at stake. The average thirty-second spot is running about $500,000. But even if you're just shooting a $25,000 spot, chances are it's a significant amount of your budget. And you feel your job is on the line.

OK, you're in LA or NYC. Perhaps even on location in some exotic place. You're getting wined and dined. It's great fun. You've met some famous people. And best of all—you're getting paid to do this.

Never forget that: *you're getting paid!* Forget about the glamour! You're job is to bring home, at the absolute minimum, the shooting board on film.

Commercials are expensive, career wrecking, and you really only have one chance when you're actually filming or taping. You can't pull the team together again. You've got to get it right the first time.

So what do you do? First, you need to recognize (if you're the client or an account executive) that you're in a foreign environment. Normally you're in the office and in control. On a set or on location you're at the mercy of other people. A shoot is the domain of the producer, director, and production company.

They're comfortable on a set or location. That's what they do for a living. It's their job to make you feel at ease, but they don't often do it. Because it's an environment they work in every day, they take it for granted you're going to be as comfortable as they are.

Wrong.

Chances are you're uncomfortable. Your ass is on the line. The budget is your responsibility. You're unfamiliar with what they're doing . . . and they're doing it in bits and pieces and often out of order.

In other words, uncomfortable is minor—hysteria is not out of the range of possibilities.

What to do?

You need to control what you must control in a mature and respectful way. Even though the shooting board has been approved by the agency, client management, and the director in the preproduction meeting, you need to again sit with the producer and director first thing while on the set and know exactly the timing and setups of how the shooting board will be produced. At that same meeting you need to discuss how alternative shots will be handled and how time might be allocated to hopefully let some "magic" happen. But the alternatives and the magic are secondary to the shooting board.

The producer and director don't know the storyboard the way you do. They were given it to bid and shoot, and even after the preproduction meeting they have their own vision of what the finished commercial will look like. That's a good thing: they can add a dimension you can't. They can bring an idea to life in remarkable ways.

Their remarkable possibilities are great and might make for a better commercial when the finished spot is delivered. But beware: Back at the office a whole bunch of people have approved a specific storyboard. The one that you and they know. You've all spent weeks (in some cases months) refining the concept and images to make what everyone thought would be the best sales message for the brand. That's what those who are paying the bill expect.

Think about having to take the rough cut back to your company. How it needs to get reapproved by everyone, including the lawyers and the networks that have already signed off on the approved storyboard version.

Instincts about changes made on the set may be right. But what if they're wrong? We've actually lost a client or two because of what we thought were minor changes on the set. Remember the ultimate approvers are hardly ever on the set. They're waiting in their offices to make the final judgments—about it and you!

They'll surely be surprised if you bring them a "magical" spot that's different. And their surprise may not be what you expect. What's been approved and what's expected is the known. Make sure you've got that before you try to be a hero.

Here's a list of several other critical things to remember on the set:

- The producer and director are in charge, so when you see something that is wrong and need to speak up, say it out of sound range of the folk who report to them and in a cool and respectful way.
- Make sure the set design is right and exactly as it was approved.
- If it looks like time is being wasted on the set and you're off to a slow shooting start, ask the producer and director about timing, overtime issues, and how to get things back on track.
- Make sure the lighting is right. Look through the camera and don't just give an automatic OK. (Jeff once had to work through a reshoot because the magnificent dining room table used in the furniture polish commercial looked like it was painted black when the film was developed. Clearly the lighting was wrong.) Don't miss that step.
- Never get the talent upset. Positive and optimistic is the needed tone.
- Keep track of what is being shot and where you are in the process. Always have the shooting board in

your hand and make notes on it. Think through the approval process and the bosses/clients who had comments and issues with the commercial. Be sure you have the answers for the questions that might be brought up again, but this time with film in hand.

Good luck. And maybe some time in the future you'll be able to enjoy a bit more of the glamour.

49

Let the People You
Hired Do Their Jobs

STEVE WAS ON THE SET OF THE FIRST COMMERCIAL HE WAS
supposed to be in charge of. His boss had come along to keep
an eye on things. They're setting up the cameras for the final
product shot. The director of photography looks in the camera lens and says "perfect." He nods to the director who looks
in the lens and says "very nice," and invites the producer to
take a look. The producer looks through the lens, says "great,"
and asks the art director to take a look. The art director looks
through the lens, says "beautiful," and invites Steve's boss to
take a look. His boss looks through the lens, smiles and turns
to Steve. "You want to take a look?" Steve said, "No." Everyone
was surprised. His boss asked, "Why not?"

Steve answered, "What if I don't like it?"

A general directs and leads. He doesn't sit in the foxhole
with the privates telling them how to aim. He doesn't sit with
the majors telling them how to execute their specialties.

The best thing you can do as a manager is let the people
you hired do their jobs. Whether it's your own staff or outside
suppliers, don't tell them how to do their jobs. If you hired
them because of their expertise, give them the opportunity to
deliver that expertise to you. The most obvious place we see

this is on a commercial shoot. It's amazing how many times we see people try to step in and micromanage the set.

The director of the commercial doesn't know your product—and you don't know how to direct a commercial. Stop telling him what you want beyond what was agreed to at the preproduction meeting. Actors don't know your product as well as you do—and you don't know how to help them reach into their emotional core and translate that onto film and into a successful communication. Stop giving them "line readings." Just listen to the words and make sure they're pronouncing the words correctly.

When you're on a set you're out of your element. It's time to let the people you've hired—the experts—do their job. And if you haven't hired experts then you haven't done your job. Gulp, shame on you. But it's probably too late to correct that error while you're shooting.

No one's telling you to be in another country when the shoot happens. Yes, it's ultimately your responsibility and you should watch carefully so you know if you have to step in at some point . . . but don't do it unless you absolutely, positively have to. (Here, "have to" means because of legal/fact/honesty/financial issues or because of incredible misuse of talent.)

If you do have to step in, the first place to go is to your producer, discreetly. Ideally, ask the producer to step outside or into another room. Even though everyone is focused on the shoot, they're also watching you out of the corner of their eye. If they sense any concerns or misgivings, it's going to start making everyone edgy. Once you've taken the producer aside, quietly discuss (no haranguing) your concerns, always relating them to the agreements made at the preproduction meeting. (Aha, now you know how important the preproduction meeting is and why you should take extensive notes.)

Be specific. Shooting sets breed insecurity and insecurity breeds failed commercials. So sit back, pretend to relax, and set the tone for the entire shoot. No one wants to go into battle led by a commanding general who looks nervous. Yes, there's a lot of money at stake and yes, your reputation is at risk, but the time to have worried about that is during all the preproduction meetings. As we describe in the next chapter, let the people you hired make some magic.

Everyone on the set has done his or her job before. You hired them for that very reason. So give them the room to make a contribution to your company. Some thoughts for you to take to the shoot:

- Give the experts some breathing room.
- Take the role of mediator and breathing room expert. (Keep yourself under control; keep the client under control if you're the agency account supervisor; keep the account executive learning, not doing.)

- Listen intently. Don't let a possible diamond of an idea from the talent or director pass without action. One of us had a boss who would never let his employees speak when an outside vendor was presenting. His point of view was simple, direct, and smart: "I can get your opinion anytime," he'd tell us. "These people are here to give us their thinking for the next hour or so; let's hear what they have to say."

- Use the preproduction meeting for all it's worth. If you're a "suit" and reading this chapter makes you nervous and makes you break out into a sweat, Jeff agrees with you. The fact that you're not in control on the set is unsettling. Especially since it's your ass on the line. The key is the preproduction meeting. That's the time to micromanage the process. That's your control area. Make sure you leave that meeting with all issues resolved and a clear action list for all involved.

A couple of words about delegating authority and feeling comfortable with that delegation are clearly in order:

1. Hire people who make you comfortable enough to laugh.
2. Hire people who like you and respect the job you do.

3. Listen to the people you hire. The more you listen, the better the job that they'll do for you.
4. Show confidence in your people. Confidence almost always leads to greater creativity and that's crucial to helping them make magic.

In short? Be a general, not a general nuisance.

50

Allow for the
Possibility of Magic

WE'RE SHOOTING A COMMERCIAL FOR SONY THAT'S SET IN A bar. Three principals are arguing about the best video camera and the bartender's quietly wiping glasses behind them and then has to interject one punchline comment. We had cast the principals when the director mentioned he knew a good, young kid who'd be perfect for the bartender. Since it wasn't a key role, we never even asked to audition him.

On the day of the shoot, the kid playing the bartender started upstaging all the actors. With a snort, a wry comment, a snide aside, he ate the principal actors for lunch—and turned a solid commercial into an award winner. (Along the way, of course, he managed to upgrade himself from "extra" to "principal.") The actor was a very young Nathan Lane.

This tip is really Part 2 of Let the People You Hired Do Their Jobs. (Also refer to Tip #18, Guide and Manage . . .)

Allowing for the possibility of magic isn't easy. It takes courage, confidence, and maturity. It's also based on two additional skills:

1. Your ability to hire the right people. Learn to develop the skill of hiring the best and you'll avoid the

scourge of mediocrity. And that scourge in this age of media fragmentation and lower audiences is just a colossal waste of money. We all have a tendency to call the most expensive or most well-known vendors. But are you calling them because they're the best—or because you're covering your ass? If you're using a tried-and-true vendor because you want to have someone to blame if things go wrong, then you're not giving yourself the benefit of the best. Trust your instincts: if you think a supplier/director/actor/vendor could really deliver the goods for you, then give them a shot—even if they're not the usual suspects.

2. Your ability to give people a little room and support in doing their jobs. Not only will they often give you more than you asked for, they'll likely go the extra distance because they'll feel less pressure . . . and that usually results in magic happening. This is especially true in the production process of a commercial (TV or Internet) or a corporate video.

The possibility of magic is based on an outside resource—actor, producer, director, editor, programmer—seeing something in the storyboard or film that neither you nor your client realized. And what they see is the opportunity to make a commercial far better than the one approved.

The first thing we do is call all the lawyers (with apologies to William Shakespeare). The key to letting magic happen is knowing you can reach corporate counsel on the day of the shoot. Your commercial has been approved by the legal department of the ad agency, the client, and the networks. Changing words can be a disaster. Speak to your attorneys, let them know you're shooting, and make sure you know how to contact them from the set. That way, if magic happens, you can call the lawyers and make sure you're not changing the legal meaning of the commercial.

How does magic happen? How it happens is truly magic—even if you follow our "rules." One really never knows. It either does or doesn't and it's often just fate—up to the advertising gods. But there's a better chance it'll happen if you let the people you hired do their job.

How often does magic happen? Not very. But you would be surprised how often it happens to the same people. That's because they have a knack for hiring the right people to shoot a particular commercial—a great skill. A skill based on an innate sense of and love of the business.

Here's how the magic may happen with each of the "players" noted above.

The actor: Actors often read and deliver lines with a different understanding than even the most attuned writers. Listen when an actor has an opinion on changing a line or reading it with a different inflection. He or she is often right. And when he's right, the change can make a huge difference in how a line is heard and how it's remembered and even acted upon. Time and time again we see actors turn what seem to be mundane lines into memorable ones that actually get picked up in the lexicon of the target audience. Now that's a win!

Often it starts with the auditioning actors demonstrating their range and bringing their unique skills to your commercial. Never underestimate the importance of a casting session. Never, ever settle for actors that won't make the spot "sing." Money spent on a second session pales in comparison to money wasted because of a boring, flat commercial.

The producer: Listen to your producer. She's an expert who knows the local talent and the production company that can make your commercial magic. We often find that a strong gut feeling by a producer for a certain actor or a particular production company pays off with an outstanding commercial. Sure it may cost a bit more, but if the storyboard can be made into a more memorable and effective commercial, the money will be really well spent. (A warning: avoid the producer that hires the same talent and production company time and time again. That won't lead to magic, it will lead to boredom—and occasionally, yikes, kickbacks.)

Today many if not most producers are freelancers. That's the good news, that's the bad news. The good news is usually driven by the independent and fresh ideas of the producer.

The bad news is usually driven by the lack of intense responsibility because of the independence. Make sure the producer you hire is totally committed to your company and has the highest standards.

The director: The most profound magic will come from hiring a director who shows a true understanding of the product, the strategy, and a love for the storyboard and a clear desire to make it even better. More than any single player in the process the director can make the biggest difference in the production of a commercial. Here are three things to look for while screening the director who can make magic happen.

1. He asks pertinent, commonsense questions about the product and the storyboard in the bidding process and listens to the answers.
2. He's involved even before the preproduction meeting and offers an altered storyboard, but one that is on strategy, on budget, and maintains the key selling message.
3. He's known to have complete control on the set and runs a tight ship so he can shoot the storyboard several different ways and still remain on time and on budget.

The editor: Let him play. If an editor gets really involved in a commercial he can often take you in a direction that even the best agency, client, and director didn't see at first blush. Editors can generate surprise, clarity, and poignancy, all major pluses in the world of commercials. Some editors don't want to see the footage until the commercial's shot. Others sometimes prefer to be on the set. Don't bar anyone from the set because of "accepted practices." Go with your gut.

By the way, when you truly understand great editing you'll be very conscious of it in almost every movie that you watch. You'll be surprised at how often you wind up saying, "The editing was incredible, and it really made a difference."

One way of helping to assure a fresh editing perspective is to give the director and editor the opportunity of a first cut. Don't put together a time schedule that allows two shooting days, two editing days, and two weeks for client approval. Give the director and editor time to sit with the film and make something special. As any good director or editor will tell you, "Film changes in the can." Things you didn't see on the set magically appear when you're watching the dailies. And, conversely, things you thought you saw on the set magically disappear in the dailies. Understand that will happen. When you're screening the first cut, don't interrupt by asking, "Can I see all the takes of that shot?" Take some time to digest what you saw, praise the work involved, and think about what you feel is both *missing* and *added*. Start by talking about the good things—the ideas and images that were added. Then move on to what you think was missing.

The programmer: (She's not on the set but a player in Internet production.) Programming is the most difficult job we have encountered. The zeros and ones of the digital world demand perfection. Close isn't good enough. We've found programmers to not only have first-rate minds but to be incredibly inquisitive and creative souls. Listen to her ideas, let her develop her concepts, encourage her understanding of the selling process. In our minds there are few things more frustrating than an annoying pop-up or crawl. So if a top-notch programmer can make your video more friendly, more watchable, and more effective, let her do it.

In summary, how do you create the environment for magic to happen? Give your resources enough time to think about what you want and what they've been hired to do. Then listen, discuss, and give them more than a bit of their head.

51

Leave an Open Mike to the Voice-over Talent

HOW MANY TAKES DO YOU NEED TO GET YOUR VOICE-OVER TV or radio announcer to nail the script? If it's more than five, something's not right.

Why? Think about this:

Voice-over announcers have a lot of experience reading advertising copy. The best ones understand selling message, audience, selling proposition, and all the other things that are needed to deliver a reading that's spot-on (as the British like to say). What they don't understand are statements like "can you read that with more feeling?"

Hey, we just wrote that sentence and *we* don't understand it.

Think about the recording experience from the point of view of the guy or gal in the booth. He's beaten out ten or twenty other professionals for the job. He's shown up ready to prove you made the right choice. You remind him of the direction. He goes into the booth. The sound engineer does a level check and then says, "Let's lay one down." The guy does a terrific reading of the script on the second or third try (after his lips are limber). And then he stands there. Alone. In the booth. Silence! No immediate feedback. All he sees through the soundproof glass are the agency people and the client all huddled together and talking. Maybe gesturing. Maybe arguing. He doesn't know. He's just standing there. He has no idea whether they're saying, "This is the greatest announcer I've ever heard" or "Who hired this loser?" or "Where are we having lunch?"

And then the producer gets on the intercom and says something totally inane like, "Can you do that with more feeling?" or, "Can you do that again but warmer?"

Huh?

The way to a fast, professional, and superb voice-over recording session is to tell the client, the producer, the voice-over talent, and the studio engineer that the intercom mike needs to remain open between the control room and the recording booth between takes.

The open mike does three critical things:

1. It lets the VO announcer hear what you think is missing or what the issues are.
2. It causes people who were going to make an unnecessary, caustic, or insipid comment to keep their mouths shut.
3. It makes the announcer part of the solution. No questions, no worries, no concerns in the recording booth.

It works. Every time. The direction is in the open and that should give you a successful recording session in three or four takes. Five to six if you want some quirky or off-the-wall ones to think about when you do the editing.

And while you're at it, think about saying "thank you." Even though you're paying the announcer. Compliments are the grease that lubricates the advertising business. A simple "thank you," or "nice job" can go a long way to breaking even the worst news. Maybe the Japanese have the right idea: anything that's not "yes" means "no." Which lets you say no a thousand different ways: "Great effort." ("Nope.") "You really went the distance." ("No.") "We appreciate all you did." ("Hated it.") Creative people have no idea where their skills come from. They operate under the constant, unexpressed fear that their talent might disappear at any moment. The most effective way you can work with creative people is to start with a compliment. Even if you're planning to stick a knife in their back, the compliment serves as an anesthetic.

The worst thing you can do is a remote voice-over session. In this age of digital high-speed communication, announcers can be in a studio in their house on Cape Cod and still "attend" a recording session. Don't do it.

We learned how important this subject is in a series of recording sessions that a client of ours had with an under-contract voice-over talent who worked from his house. Ugly.

It put the talent in complete control of the process. To this day, we still don't know where his head was, but it wasn't in the sessions and doing the best job possible. But when he said, "Done," and hung up, there was little the client could do.

The commercials suffered—and no one (except the talent) was pleased with the results.

Where the hell were the client's priorities? The dollar savings amounted to perhaps $3,000 in travel costs. The time saving was one-half day. The loss that was suffered was unmeasurable—the loss of effectiveness of the commercial.

We wondered how much less product the commercials sold. Probably a hell of a lot less than $3,000. And we could clearly see that working long-distance corroded the level of quality sought (and given) in much of the client's work. Average became good enough. And that probably affected millions of dollars in potential sales.

Leaving an open mike to the talent and having them present in the studio both add up to the same thing: voice-over announcing is a "need-to-be-there" process. It's an essential part of the communications to make the sale.

Once you're at the session, what should happen? Well, first of all, the tone of the reading should have been discussed and agreed to at the preproduction meeting. Second, the talent should be reminded of what is being sought before she walks into the recording booth. And then, as we've noted in earlier chapters, you should let the experts do their job—but this time with one exception: unlike being quiet on the set, we again suggest that you open the mike from the control room to the recording booth and let the talent hear what is going on between takes. Let her understand just what the issues are.

In summary:

- Prepare for the recording session at the preproduction meeting.
- Have everyone attend the recording session—at the studio.
- Keep an open mike at the recording session.
- Keep the talent informed so he can be part of the solution.

Managing communication between you and the voice-over talent looks like you're staying in control. But it's too short a leash. Keep an open mike—and an open mind—and let the talent do their job.

52

Don't Leave Issues to Be Solved in the Editing Room

EDITING IS ONE OF THE MOST IMPORTANT ASPECTS OF THE advertising process. But be warned—"we'll fix it in the mix" is the biggest production sin of all.

If something's not working on a shoot or in a recording session, STOP, IMMEDIATELY! Take a breath. Take a break and think about what isn't working. Pull your team together and figure out what's wrong and how you can fix it right there and then.

Does this tip contradict Tip #48 (Let the People You Hired Do Their Jobs)? Not if you're in control of yourself. Yes, you might have concerns. Those should be discussed with the producer. But sometimes the concern might be more than minor. If you've hired the right producer he can decide whether to bring more people into the discussion. At some point it will be clear to everyone that there's a serious disagreement. If that point is reached, the smartest, most economical thing to do is take a break and get everyone back on track.

If you're not comfortable, chances are it's an internal, subconscious signal coming from your experience. Trust yourself. Be smart. Act. Don't sit there like a lump and depend on others.

Even if it will take a number of calls to your bosses, perhaps the lawyers, and your clients . . . that's okay. Just make sure that you can explain the situation accurately and quickly and provide the proposed solution in a clear and concise manner so that you can get new approvals and move ahead with the fix.

Yes, the meter will be running. Yes, there will be lots of commotion on the set or in the studio, but it's a lot cheaper (with a lot less agita) to solve a problem at the time it comes up than having to work around it later and provide excuse after excuse.

How do you solve the problem at the set? Again, pull together your working team. Ask "What's wrong?" "Why isn't this working?" Make sure everyone is honest and open and listen, listen, listen to their input.

If everyone is trying to convince you that it's not a problem, keep an open mind—but don't necessarily cave in. Your job is to make sense of what is being said and to formulate a plan of action, not to go with the loudest or most forceful voice.

Remember that everyone on the set has their own agenda. There will be tremendous pressure on you—after all, the clock is ticking and money is flowing—but at the end of the day you've got to be sure you're comfortable and convinced that moving ahead, with whatever decision is made, is the right decision. After all, you've got to answer for the decision made. The vendors will be long gone, perhaps never to be seen again.

We believe that a ten-minute or even thirty-minute break can translate into a huge financial and emotional savings down the road. Be smart and be cost effective. Don't let something slide if you're not 100 percent comfortable. If you're not comfortable, chances are that your boss or your client won't be either. That's why you've got to act immediately. Don't put yourself in the "now what" situation, after the set has been struck and it's too late to make any changes without enormous costs.

If you've got concerns, express them. Listen to everyone's input. If they're right, they're saving you and will make you look like a hero. If they're wrong, but clearly want to push ahead, then make it clear who'll pay for the reshoot. Ninety-nine percent of the time that will stop them—or at least get you the extra take(s) ("your way") that the editor and your bosses might thank you for the next day.

BONUS

"I'll quit when it stops being fun."

So those are the tips we think are most important. Culled from some 200 we've accumulated over the years. Think of them as a graduate program in marketing and advertising—what to do after you know everything there is to do.

There's one last thought we want to leave you with. In the heat of battle, it's often the hardest one to remember . . . but the most important one of all.

53
Have Fun

THIRTY-FIVE YEARS AGO, IN HIS AUTOBIOGRAPHICAL BOOK on advertising, Jerry Della Femina noted, "Advertising is the most fun you can have with your clothes on." Well, maybe in the '60s and '70s . . .

But even though it's gotten a lot harder, it's still not "work."

There's no heavy lifting.

You get to be indoors in all kinds of weather.

You get to imagine and create things that never existed before.

Occasionally you get to fly to strange, exotic places like Cleveland.

In all, it sure beats the hell out of working for a living.

When you're caught in the daily grind of deadlines and bullshit, it's often easy to forget that simple truth. If you do forget it, step back, take a deep breath, and think about what kind of job you could get with your skill set if you weren't in advertising.

Scary, huh?

Immerse yourself in life.

Be yourself.

Study people.

Enjoy today's culture.

Love other people's advertising.

Embrace all of life's experiences and bring it back to your office every Monday morning.

In short? Enjoy life. Advertising is one of the few arenas that requires you to have as much fun as you can. It makes you a better salesperson. It makes you a better creative person. And it makes you a better person to be around.

So get out there and have some fun. You've earned it. You deserve it. And you're in a job where it's actually required!

Acknowledgments

Jeff Woll

To Adrian Zackheim, who encouraged us to write the book and guided us to an informative read that will, hopefully, generate smiles.

To our editor, Adrienne Schultz, who had the patience to work with a "Mars Jeff" and a "Venus Steve" through the rewrites.

This book could not have been written without the professional and life teachings of my coworkers at Ogilvy, but in particular:

the late David Ogilvy, whose brilliant leadership led me to my love of advertising and management and whose uncharacteristic advice about family helped shape my life.

Bill Whitney, who taught me how to be an account executive but, far more important, a better person.

Joel Raphaelson, who successfully shared his love of writing and advertising. I trust he thinks I learned.

Raymonde Lavoie, who reinvigorated my love of exciting creative work and proved that the best could become a cultural happening.

To every creative team I worked with who made me look smarter than I am.

To every client that had trust in me and our creative teams.

To Jennifer Stewart, Michael Grandfield, and Peter Wolf, my partners at Red Shark Technology, who opened my eyes to the wonders of the computer and how it could change advertising.

To the late Geoffrey Frost, who was a great supporter of Red Shark's technology and me.

To Norm Siegel, the most rational and persuasive art director I have worked with.

To Steve Lance, my coauthor, who is a great listener, writer, supporter, partner, and friend.

Steve Lance

They say writers are born, not made. It's been my experience that writers are made, not born. And if you're lucky, like I was, there's no shortage of good people who are willing to share their knowledge and experience and help make you a great writer.

Special thanks to Adrian Zackheim, who read everything we sent him, offered encouragement, and kept saying, "I'm still waiting for your book . . ."

To our editor, Adrienne Schultz, who kept us focused on the goal.

To my brother, Paul, the real writer in the family.

To my mother, Ethel, the librarian, who infused in us the love of the written word.

To the late George Shaver, a Zen master of business, who taught me more in eighteen months than I've learned before and since.

To Chris Moseley and Jane Maas—who respected my talent, tolerated my personality, and kept asking, "So when are you going to write a book?"

To Christos Cotsakos, who gambled on an untried author and gave me free rein to bring his vision to life.

To my partner, Norman Siegel, who constantly reminds me I'm not the best writer he's ever worked with—but still hasn't quit.

To my partner and coauthor, Jeff Woll, who insisted on "process," kept us on schedule, and truly made this book happen.

To Carole Schweid, who kept asking, "Where's the heart?"

To Nancy Winston, who keeps asking, "Yes, but what's the point?"

To Lisa Selwitz, who insisted on teaching an old dog new tricks.

To Kelly Monaghan, a brilliant raconteur, a great travel companion, and the first published author I ever met.

To Richard Kahn, who showed me where the edges were and never let me win a game of Scrabble.

To Norman Tanen, who was always willing to put up with me and was willing to try anything—including going along for the ride.

And most of all to Roger Feldman, who took the time to start from zero and take a chance on a wet-behind-the-ears kid fresh out of college without a clue what he wanted to do in life. And while Roger might say, "It wasn't me," he and I both know it was.

Biographies

Steve Lance is a partner at Unconventional Wisdom, a creative resource group located on the Internet at uwisdom.com. He was previously a creative director with the entertainment division of Della Femina, Travisano & Partners, and creative director of NBC, and has won numerous industry awards throughout his career.

Jeff Woll was a twenty-year veteran of Ogilvy & Mather, including stints as COO of its Montreal office (where his team won seven gold medals in Quebec's Agency of the Year awards); CEO of Ogilvy & Mather Partners in New York; and senior vice president of corporate development for North America. He is currently a partner at Unconventional Wisdom.

We'd love to hear from you. For questions, comments, suggestions, and feedback, e-mail us at LittleBlueBook@uwisdom.com.